# Holy

# Happenings

## Evidence of God's Faithfulness

# Endorsements

Holy Happenings is a book of vignettes, snapshots into God's work in a person's life. It's about the amazing detail God puts into guiding and crafting our lives. Each vignette reveals another aspect of God's character and how it affects our daily life as His child. As you read, you will laugh, cry and see God through Norma's life - enjoy!

Rev. Douglas Rabe, Superintendent
The Harvest Conference Free Methodist Church

Holy Happenings takes you on a delightful stroll through a lifetime of walking hand-in-hand with Jesus! The reader will be awed at the examples of God's faithfulness - in plenty and in want. Norma's story is a refreshing testimony that "Nothing is too difficult for Christ!"

Cynthia Cucinotta,
author of Vignettes from the Vine

# ACKNOWLEDGMENTS

I am so grateful to all those who have prayed for me and encouraged me to write this book.

Debby - Your invaluable help and guidance have made the publishing process possible and a joy. God blessed me when He brought you into my life!

Eucelia - I am so grateful God allowed our paths to cross! Not only has He gifted you with an anointed voice as you sing for Him and to Him, you are a skilled editor.

Jean D. - Your faithful prayers and your love for Jesus inspire me and make you shine!

Tish - You are one of my most faithful prayer intercessors. I can always count on you. I thank God for you!

Pastor Doug - Your unwavering integrity and your commitment to the Lord have profoundly impacted my walk with the Lord through the years! You set the bar high!

Arlene - You pray, but along with those prayers, you live out your faith in so many ways! I am deeply grateful for the times you have given up your home for our use on several occasions, be it for a retreat or a place for us to stay while work was being done on our home.

My CBS family - Studying God's Word with you has made my life so much richer!

My church family - I love worshipping our Lord with you!

My Ladies of Grace sisters and my Movie club sisters - Each of you has a very special place in my life and in my heart!

Cynthia - Your encouragement and willingness to preview what I wrote and letting me "bounce" things off you have been such a blessing, as has our relationship!

Wanda - Your sweet spirit and giving heart have blessed me in so many ways! You are a treasure!

Will and Linda - our traveling companions, both on the literal highway and on the road of life - It's such a joy to be able to share our mutual love for our Lord as we pray, laugh and play together.

Ellie and Kathy, my Aaron and Hur - We have shared so much through the years, the good and the not so good, but especially our growth in our Lord Jesus! Having both of you as lifetime sisters in Him has graced my life beyond measure!

Tisa and Dave, Brian and Liz, Greg and Kerry - I am incredibly blessed by all each of you adds to our family!

Aidan, Maddi, David, Eli, Abby, Leah, Chloe - You bring such unparalleled joy into my life as I watch each of you grow into who God made you to be!

Al - You have prayed for me and cheered me on every step of the way as I went from jotting down ideas to finishing the manuscript, and you have gone "above and beyond" by taking over household chores so I could devote all of my time to writing.

Whenever I share something I feel God is telling me to do, you always say, "If God told you to do it, then you need to do it." You never question it!  It is so easy to see Christ in you!  My love for you just keeps getting stronger through the years, and I never cease thanking God for the gift you are!

Most of all, my Heavenly Father - I treasure Your daily presence and Your love and care for me.  Thank you for giving me eyes to see Your hand in all that happens in my life.  It's all for Your glory!

# Dedication

This book is lovingly dedicated to my family:

Al, my God-given soul-mate

My children and their spouses

My precious grandchildren

I love you all so much and thank God for every one of you!

I will praise You, Oh Lord,
with all my heart, I will tell of
all Your wonders.
Psalm 9:1 (NIV)

# Contents

# Introduction

## God With Us

Traveling through this life is a journey. We find straight roads, sharp turns, dips into valleys and paths up to such heights where the beauty is almost indescribable. There is one constant throughout the journey, though. That is God's presence with us. As we travel, our goal should be to get closer to God.

As I look back on my life, I can see He has been right with me, His hand directing and guiding every step I have taken. He is my Creator. He made me and knows every intricate detail of who I am. I praise Him because "…I am fearfully and wonderfully made" Psalm 139:14 (NIV). God tells Moses in Exodus 33:12 that He knows him by name. He also knows us by name.

I love the words of the song, *"He Knows My Name" by Tommy Walker:*

> "I have a Maker.
> He formed my heart.
> Before even time began,
> my life was in His hands."

If we let these words sink deep within us, we realize the incredible specialness of the Lord's relationship with us. I'm nobody special in the eyes of the world, but I'm somebody special in the eyes of God! I am His child, as are you. That makes us royalty - we are children of the King! I am a daughter of the King, a princess! Do you see yourself as a beloved child of the King, made in His image?

In Acts 10:34 (NIV), Peter said, "how true it is that God does not show favoritism." God made every one of us, and He works in every life whether or not we realize or acknowledge it. Dr. Mark Hanby says, "When we become awakened to God's desire and love, we see that He is constantly doing amazing things, even when we fail to notice."

He is our Father who loves us and longs for a close relationship with us. He desires to provide for every one of us, to protect us and to be present in each of our lives. And knowing that He wants His best for us should encourage us to trust Him with our lives. But just as earthly parents need to treat each of their children as unique individuals, so too, God's best for me may be different from His best for you. Just trust Him. He makes no mistakes.

Since the beginning of time, God has communicated with His people. He spoke to Adam and Eve in the garden. He spoke to Moses through the burning bush, to Joseph though a dream, and to Elijah through a whisper. God is the same God today. When we accept Jesus as our Savior, He comes to live in us in the form of the Holy Spirit. The Holy Spirit is God in us, and He speaks to us in many ways. He has spoken to me as a voice in my spirit, through His Word, the Bible, through other people, dreams, songs and circumstances, and even through a vision. Job 33:13 (NIV) says, "For God does speak, now one way, now another."

In order to clearly hear God's voice, we need to spend time in His presence. When we do, we experience a stillness in our spirits that enables us to hear Him. This quiet time is something we need every single day. It is vital to me that I start my day with it. St. Augustine is quoted as praying, "My Father, I will quiet my soul now and enter into its sanctuary with You." Jesus says, "My sheep hear My voice…" John 10:27 (KJV).

The Good Shepherd

Stop and listen to what He has to say. Sit at His feet, and listen with your heart. Quiet your mind, removing all thoughts rolling around in there. He will speak to you, and you will hear Him if you truly listen. One caution, though. When you think you are hearing God's voice, be sure what you are hearing lines up with His Word. If it goes against what He says in the Bible, that voice is not from Him.

One should always look for the spiritual significance of a happening, as well as listening for His voice. He orchestrates so many happenings for our growth in faith, and we don't want to miss those.

God has provided us with all that we need to walk this journey. First, we should remember that God knows the way through the wilderness. All we have to do is follow. The greatest guide of all is His Word, the Bible, the road map for our lives as we travel on the highway to Heaven. The most wonderful realization is that He is the same God today that He was in the beginning of time and throughout the days of the Old Testament. Really the only difference is that in Old Testament times, God dwelled <u>with</u> His people. Since God sent Jesus to earth to die for our sins and left us the Holy Spirit, God now dwells <u>within</u> His people. We can expect and look forward to His involvement in our lives just as He was intimately involved in the lives of Abraham, Sarah, Moses, David, John, Paul, Peter and so many others of Biblical times.

Now come with me as I take you along on my life's journey.

# Chapter 1

# Salvation

## The Early Years

I grew up in a small resort town right on the water in Upstate New York. My parents divorced at a time when divorce was quite uncommon. In fact, when I went to school, I was the only kid in my class from a broken home. I was two at the time of the

Mom And Me When I Was A Baby

divorce, and my mom and I moved to a nearby city. When I was five, my mom had  no one to take care of me while she worked, so she took me back to the town where I was born to be raised by my paternal grandmother. When I was ten, she remarried, and my step-father was in the service. They were stationed in many different locations so she chose to let me stay where I was. After that, there were times when I didn't see my mother for almost a year.

My father remarried and lived nearby. He would come to my grandmother's home, and I would see him almost every day. I used to curl up on his lap when I was little. I especially looked forward to my birthday each year because he would take me out for a lobster dinner. That was such a treat and I felt really special. I remember once when I was about eight-years old and was at his house, my step-mother was angry about something and threw a pan of boiling water at me. That was the last time my dad ever took me there. When I was a teen, I went to see her in the hospital. She was dying of cancer. God filled me with love and compassion, and I was able to completely forgive her. At that time, I didn't realize that was God's grace working in me.

I loved growing up by the water. We were surrounded on three sides by a bay and a lake. I learned to swim and tried water skiing, even though I wasn't very good at that. I pretty much lived outside all summer. My best friend and I slept in tents we made from chenille bedspreads draped over the clothesline and secured with clothespins as stakes hammered into the ground. We were rarely in the house! We used to swing on a tire hanging from a tree, and we would climb the mulberry tree in

the yard, picking and eating the yummy berries.

In autumn, we rode our bikes and made leaf houses, laying out all the rooms like a big blueprint on the ground. During winter, we would sled down the hill and skate on the frozen bay. It was a good life, an idyllic one in so many ways. But oh, how I missed

my mom! She came to see me regularly before she remarried, and when she would leave, I would literally get what I used to call a "lump" in my throat and be so sad. I would go in my closet and cry.

As far back as I can remember, though, God was real to me. My faith as a child was unquestioning. Even though I couldn't see God, I knew in my heart that He existed. In my sadness, I felt His presence, even at that young age, and I can remember turning to Him for comfort. My aunt, who also lived with my grandmother, gave me my first Bible when I was nine. My grandmother did the best she could and took care of me physically, but she was never emotionally present. She had come to America from Italy as a young wife, and she spoke broken English. She was completely deaf and couldn't read lips or understand sign language, so the only way to communicate with her was to shout into her ear.

As a teen, I would spend hours sitting on a cliff down by the lake, writing poetry or journaling my thoughts and dreams for my future. When I was twelve, my grandmother was in the hospital recovering from surgery. She had a nurse who was very harsh with her, and I witnessed it. That, and the fact my mom, whom I looked up to, was a nurse, led to my decision to become a nurse. I was determined to be kind and caring to patients, rather than harsh and mean like that nurse had been to my grandmother. Upon graduating from high school, I went on to nursing school and became an RN.

I really never got into any kind of trouble growing up, mainly for two reasons. First, I prayed a very simple prayer every night asking God to help me do the right thing and be who He wanted me to be. He answered that prayer. And, I had a very healthy fear of my earthly father, who was the chief of police in our town!

We are not to dwell on the past, but God can and does use our past experiences for our good. Oswald Chambers said, "Beware of going back to what you once were when God wants you to be something you have never been."

## Salvation Comes to Our Home

I grew up going to church, and I believed in God and wanted to please Him, but I didn't have a personal relationship with Jesus. I know now that nothing else really matters except knowing Him personally. I really met Jesus on a retreat when I was in my twenties and married with two children. It was designed for husbands to go first and wives at a later date. When my husband, Al went, he came home changed. He began reading his Bible every day, and I could see that he was growing in his faith. I wanted what he had found, so I went with great anticipation. Jeremiah 29:13 (NAS) says, "You will seek Me and find Me when you search for Me with all your heart." However, by the end of the first day, I was discouraged because I felt no different.

That evening, I knelt by my bed and prayed. It was then that I heard a voice in my spirit say, "Get a pen and a piece of paper." I did, and I knelt back down. Immediately, words began to flow from the pen to the paper. When they stopped, I looked at what I had written:

"Hold my hand, Lord Jesus, and walk by my side.
I love You, Lord Jesus, and I'll no longer hide
From trial or tribulation, from sorrow or pain
I love You, Lord Jesus, in sunshine and rain.

You gave Your life for me, yet I've turned away
From the anguish of Your suffering, but starting today,

With Your love to guide me each step of the
way,
I'll follow You, Lord Jesus, and do
whatever You say."

As I read it, I remember thinking, "Oh,
no. I can't do that. I'm not there," but by
the end of the weekend, I surrendered my
life to the Lord and began my spiritual
journey.

The retreat was held at a retreat center
overlooking a lake. The weekend pro-
gressed, and it was noon that Saturday. I
was standing outside looking out at the
water when I saw an emergency vehicle
across the lake, traveling down the road with
its lights flashing. I felt God was saying,
"Follow Me." At that moment, I was finally
able to "own" what I had written in that
prayer. My response was "yes, I will." How
appropriate that I was by the water, since so
many of my special "soul" times had been
and continue to be by the water! By the
way, I never had to memorize that prayer the
Holy Spirit gave me. It was indelibly
imprinted in my brain from the moment I
first read it, and it has never left me!

There was a closing service at the end of the retreat weekend, and each participant was asked to give a short synopsis of what the weekend meant to her. When it was my turn, I spoke about how I felt compelled to write, and then I shared the prayer, completely from memory. After the service ended, a man came up to me. He was quite emotional and said he believed the Lord was speaking directly to him through it.

Once I accepted Jesus as my Savior and Lord, it made all the difference in my life. I want to please Him by doing what's right in His eyes. I want to be in His perfect will. When I serve others or gain any acclaim, I want Him to get the glory. I want to be a reflection of Him! Matthew 5:16 (KJV) says, "Let your light so shine before men, that they may see your good works and glorify your Father, which is in Heaven."

When I got home from my weekend, my husband and I shared our experiences. Before that, he had kept much of what happened on his retreat from me so my weekend wouldn't be spoiled or influenced by his experience. We talked well into the night, and this was perfect timing for him to be able to relive his weekend.

Three days later in the afternoon, my mother-in-law called to say my father-in-law had suffered a massive heart attack and died. I decided to wait until Al got home from work to tell him since he would be leaving work shortly. He was spiritually "high" when he walked in, telling me he had worked all day with the man who had been the leader on his retreat. They sang songs from the weekend and just shared their faith throughout the day. He had never worked with him before (they worked for different contractors), and he never worked with him again. It was clear the Lord had planned out the day to prepare him to receive the news of his father's passing.

## "Niagara" Falls

I once heard a message about God pouring out His love for us. The pastor shared that the Greek word for "pour" is "niagara. Romans 5:5 (NIV) says, "Hope does not disappoint us, because God has poured out His love into our hearts by the

Holy Spirit whom He has given us." Think of Niagara Falls and how the water keeps overflowing and doesn't ever stop. It's endless. Now imagine God's love being "niagaraed" over us. Wow, what a concept! As we are filled to overflowing, His love should change us and then flow out from us to others. Ever since I heard that message years ago, I have always envisioned God's love for us as going on and on and on, never stopping. The same is true of His grace. He lavishes us with it. He pours,"niagaras" His grace over us, and that too, should flow out from us to others.

Speaking of Niagara Falls, that reminds me of a dear friend and how God used me in her life. This friend called one day and told me she had cancer. She and I had roomed together after we got out of nursing school, and we worked in the same hospital. We toured Europe together for four months, and after we were both married, she and her husband and Al and I would often get together. Soon after I accepted the Lord, the four of us went to Niagara Falls together. I was obnoxious! All I could talk about was Jesus, and they didn't want to hear it. After that weekend, we drifted apart, seeing each other only a couple of times a year.

I did go to see her the day after she called me with her bad news. I wanted to talk with her about having a relationship with the Lord, but there were so many interruptions - her mother came over, her neighbor stopped in, she received some phone calls. I didn't have an opportunity to really talk with her.

That night, I couldn't sleep. I kept hearing a voice say "Go to Ellie." I began to argue "I already went today," but that voice was unrelenting. Another friend and I led a Bible study that was meeting at her house the next day. It was my 40th birthday, and she had a birthday cake for me. I called her and told her about my night and apologized, saying I couldn't be there because I had to go to Ellie. I asked for her and the other ladies to pray for me. When I arrived at Ellie's, she was very surprised to see me and asked, "What are you doing here?" I told her I couldn't sleep because a voice kept telling me to "Go to Ellie." She then said, "Well, I couldn't sleep because I kept saying

'God, I want what Norma has.' " I went in and led her to the Lord. What an incredible birthday gift that was for me!

Years later, her husband accepted the Lord, and he was just as "on fire" for the Lord as I had been. One day, he said to me, "Remember when we were in Niagara Falls, and we were having dinner in that revolving restaurant? If that window opened, I think I would have thrown you out of it!" We need to be careful not to turn anyone away from the Lord and to be sensitive to where others are on their journey. We also have to be in tune with the Holy Spirit and His direction for sharing the faith we have. If we walk in His light, that light shines through us, and God will often use it to draw others to Himself.

## No More "Soaps"

As we strive to become more like Him, we need to be ready to make some changes in our lives. Because Al was gone much of the time, and I had young children, I used to look forward to soap operas. It was a "connection" with some adults! I used to send the children outside or to another room to play because I knew it was something they shouldn't see.

One day, I read an article in a magazine about a lady who looked forward to a friend coming to her house for tea every day. That friend would talk about affairs she was having, and the hostess would listen and be drawn in to the conversation. As a Christian, I remember thinking I would never do that. At the end of the article, the writer said that was what we were doing if we were watching soap operas. I stopped watching them that day and never went back to them.

1 Peter 1:15-16 (NIV) tells us "just as He who called you is holy, so be holy in all you do, for it is written, 'Be holy, because I am holy'." God is holy, and He calls us to holiness. He has given us the power to become holy in Christ. We need to realize His life within us. Thomas Moore once said, "Spirituality asks for some measure of withdrawal from a world set up to ignore soul."

# Chapter 2

# Special Homecomings and Get-Aways

Throughout our married life and while raising our kids, Al faced working in other states or places too far to travel each day. Having experienced being separated from my mom as a child, it was just as difficult, if not more so, to have my husband be away from home so much. Even though I felt alone and lonely at times, I grew in my trust of the Lord. He has always been there for me. His promise is that He will never leave us. Loved ones may not be with us for various reasons, but God is right there. He is our hope, our strength, the One we can, and should, lean on.

The kids and I always made a "big deal" over Al coming home on Friday nights when he was gone all week. We kept an index card on the refrigerator where the kids marked off each day he was away. On those Friday nights, they were allowed to

Welcoming Daddy home after a week away!

watch "Dukes of Hazzard," have soda and stay up past their bedtime so they would be up when he got home. Hearing him pull in the driveway was cause for celebration!

I missed Al terribly, but God always provided special times for us as a couple. The kids were in college or on their own in

1998 when Al was working in New Jersey. I was working at that time, so I couldn't go with him. He would come home once a month. We devised a plan so we could be together every two weeks. We found a very affordable Christian bed and breakfast between work and home and rented a room there once a month. The neatest thing about that was that there was an "overflow" house on the property when the bed and breakfast was full. We rented one room and were put there every time for the eight months Al was working in New Jersey, and we always had the entire house to ourselves. No one else ever stayed in it while we were there. Even the innkeeper credited the Lord for arranging it!

Our special get-a-way Bed and Breakfast that the Lord provided for us.

It was a beautiful newly-built log cabin with a gorgeous fireplace and a full kitchen. The innkeeper would bring our breakfast in a basket each morning and just leave it at the door. What a special, blessed time that was for us and a true gift from God!

Al worked in Maine for nine weeks, and I was able to take three weeks off to spend it with him in one of our favorite spots, on the ocean. It was off-season so he was able to rent an inexpensive efficiency apartment right across the street from the ocean. Each morning, after he left for work, I would comb the beach for shells and sand dollars. I would go down the road to the crab shack for crab or lobster rolls for lunch, and Al was able to come "home" for lunch every day. He was working on property that was right on the ocean and walking distance from our little place. That time is such a special memory, and we know God orchestrated the whole time for us.

One thing that created anxiety at that time was my traveling to Maine. I took a train, and it arrived considerably behind schedule at 2 AM in the nearby town to where Al was staying, and the stop was in a field in what seemed to be the middle of nowhere.  The conductor told me he would not let me off unless someone was there to pick me up.  This was before everyone had cell phones so I couldn't let Al know we were going to be really late.  I prayed real hard that he wouldn't think I wasn't coming and leave, but praise God, he was there waiting for me!

We both love the splendor of the ocean, and whenever I go to the ocean, I am renewed!  I especially love the crashing waves!  Psalm 93:4 (KJV) says, "The Lord on high is mightier than the noise of many waters, yea, than the mighty waves of the sea."  Think about that for a moment - there is such power as the waves come crashing onto the rocks, but God is even more powerful, more mighty!  That same God who created the ocean is the One who created us, loves us, cares and provides for us, protects us and guides us!  He is the power that is always there for us!

In 1994, our 25th anniversary celebration was even more special than our wedding had been! We had a complete ceremony in church. Our children were all involved. Our daughter did a special reading, our oldest son was the usher, and our youngest son did all the music, playing the piano and the trumpet. He even played the processional, Purcell's Trumpet Voluntary, as his dad and I walked down the aisle. That had been the piece the musician at our wedding had played as I walked down the aisle to be joined with my groom. We renewed our vows, which we had written. It could not have been more special! After the ceremony, we had a joyous celebration with our family and friends.

Renewing our vows on our 25th anniversary

A few years ago, I wrote a poem for Al for Valentine's Day. I titled it <u>Ode to Our Love</u>:

Many years ago, on a cold November day,
you stepped into my life and stole my heart away.
We courted for eleven months, then walked down the aisle.
I looked into your eyes and was captured by your smile.

Throughout the years,
we've had special times together.
We've celebrated our love with getaways
despite all kinds of weather.
We've stayed in cabins in the woods and in
inns so elegant.
It really didn't matter where we were, we
were happy in a tent.
We've cruised upon the ocean and walked
hand-in-hand along its shores.
We've seen the sunrise from the pier and
gone back for many encores.

In the midst of our busy lives, an evening
out was the perfect tonic -
dinner at a restaurant or a concert by the
Philharmonic.
A candlelight dinner by the fire when money
was a little tight
would be just what we needed and make for
a perfect night.

We've been blessed with so much love
and a beautiful family.
Throughout the years, our love has grown,
and you are the world to me.
Our faith in God has seen us through some
trials and some tears.

We know without Him in our lives, we'd be
full of doubts and fears.
He's given us each other,
and that makes our life worthwhile.
As we grow old together, I'm still captured
by your smile.

A little aside, Al
proposed to me just
two weeks after we
met, and I said
"yes." God had
picked us for each
other!

Al and Me in 1969

We often go to
the lake to watch
the sun set. Each
one is different and
showcases God's
magnificence. "At
sunset, God's glory is reflected on the mirror
of the sky," says Linda Anderson . "It's a
moment when time stands still and you see
God in all His glorious beauty. And you
worship at His footstool."

We love sunsets, but we especially love to watch the sunrise - God's way of beginning each day and letting us know He is with us. We enjoy taking our coffee down to the water near where we live to watch it. We do our devotions there, at that time, too. Psalm 19:1 (NIV) says, " The heavens declare the glory of God, the skies proclaim the work of His hands." All creation seems to sing His praises, to shout His glory! My heart is usually so filled with anticipation and wonder each time I am waiting for the first glimpse of the sun peeking over the horizon.

One day, I wrote:

# <u>God's Gifts</u>

Sitting down by the pier, waiting for the sun
to rise,
We can only marvel at what's before our
eyes.
Shades of purple, pink and blue fill the skies
above.
Only God could paint such beauty. It's truly
a gift of His love.

The sky is ablaze with color. My soul is
filled with delight.
I look upon this treasure from our Creator,
and
I'm so grateful for the gift of my sight!

The sun rising every morning and setting
every night are wonderful evidences of
God's faithfulness! And, the beauty that we
see in a sunrise or a sunset and in the ocean
and the mountains are all just a hint of the
glory of what Heaven will be!

We worked as volunteers at a Christian
camp in the Adirondack Mountains one

summer. Since we were volunteers for the week, we were assigned a room. Ours was in a lodge right on the water. In fact, it looked and felt as if we were on a cruise ship because all we could see from our window was water. The sunset on the water each night was incredible! The cost of our room would have been $1400 for the week, but we didn't have to pay a penny since we were working. I really believe we got the best room in the whole camp. And, the icing on the cake was the special speaker for the week was Ravi Zacharias, one of our favorites!

One of my journal entries that week we were at camp was, "I am sitting here in our room, and I can't fully describe what I am experiencing at this moment. The CD player is on, and Gordon Mote is singing '*Don't Let Me Miss the Glory*' in the background as I am listening to the lapping of the water on the shore right outside the window. I look out at the mountains in the distance, the water directly in front of me, the sun's rays glistening like diamonds on its surface, its warmth beating on me through the window. The white billowy clouds look like fluffy cotton. It is mid-afternoon, and I am anticipating tonight's presentation by God, the Creator of all of this beauty. His sunset should be spectacular! It always is, but seeing it from our picture window here is so awesome. This place is literally at the very edge of the water. Looking out the window, all we can see in front of us is the water, no land, just the mountains on the other side of the lake. I feel like I'm on a cruise ship. Thank You, Father, for all of this beauty! How blessed I am to be here! My soul is filled to overflowing by all of it - I am totally overwhelmed by Your gifts to me, Lord!" At the end of that day, I wrote, "Each day is a gift, but today was an exceptional one! God, You are so awesome!"

Two days later, my journal entry began, "God, how awesome You are! You created the earth and everything in it, and You chose to dwell in my heart! Here at daybreak, everything is so silent and so peaceful. Lord God, fill me with Your peacefulness. Help me to be still before You, deep within my soul. I think of one of my favorite scripture verses, Psalm 46:10, 'Be still and know that I am God.' That is the caption I would put under a picture of a morning here!"

We had talked about and dreamed about going on an Alaskan Cruise with Charles Stanley. A few months before our 48th anniversary, our children were all home and asked us what we wanted for our 50th anniversary. They said they needed time so they could plan and save for it. We told them we wanted to go on that cruise. They all said we shouldn't wait, we should go then. That was in May, and the cruise would be in July. It didn't seem possible with so little time to get ready. We did look into it and made the decision to go. We had a fantastic time!

The talks, the worship, the food and the entertainment were all wonderful, but the real highlight of the trip was the day our ship "parked" in Glacier Bay with the glaciers all around us. We were standing on deck in total awe of the magnificent beauty when Dr. Stanley came over the P.A. system and began reading chapter one of Genesis. Then, he began humming "How Great Thou Art", and I think everyone there started singing it. It sounded like heavenly angels. It was as if we had died and gone to Heaven. It is definitely a memory I will cherish forever!

Glacier Bay, Alaska

# Chapter 3

# God in the Big Things

If we keep our eyes open every day, looking for the Lord's hand in everything that happens, we will find Him there! Dwight L. Moody said, "If our circumstances find us in God, we will find God in all our circumstances." Dr. Hanby says, "To heighten your sensitivity to spiritual things, look for the hand of God in all that happens in your life." Also, he describes what some may call coincidences as "God's timing intersecting with His purpose." They are

really much more than just coincidence.
They are divine occurrences.

## Nativity Set

In 1969, the first Christmas we were
married, Al and I bought an inexpensive
nativity set at the grocery store. It was a
creche with all of the figures securely
attached to it. Only the little rooftop section
came off. A few years later, I thought we
needed a more elaborate set, so I bought a
set with all individual ceramic figures. I put
our original one out to sell in a garage sale.
An elderly woman bought it, and as she
walked down our driveway with her
purchase, I was immediately sorry I had sold
it. It was our very first nativity! It had
sentimental value! The woman's daughter
was our neighbor, so the next time I saw her,
I mentioned that if her mother ever decided
she no longer wanted it, I would gladly buy
it back.

Years went by. We had moved to another
town, the woman passed away and her
husband went to a nursing home, where he
later passed away. One day, I received a

phone call from the daughter, telling me she would like to stop by. She came to my house and gave me back that nativity set. She told me her dad had used it each of the Christmases while he was in the nursing home, and she felt real bad because the top piece was missing. I was so blessed to have it back, even without the top piece, but it is now even more special than ever because my husband made a new roof top for it. That nativity set is one of my most prized possessions today!

Our first Nativity

## Plaid Shorts

It was a very hot, very humid day when we went to visit some cousins. They lived near a creek, so we took lawn chairs to the creek and put them right in the water. The water wasn't deep, but the current was very swift. We had two very young children at the time, a four-year old daughter and a two-year old son. They had a three-year old son. The three of them sat at our feet splashing and playing as the adults visited. Things can happen so suddenly, and one might not even notice, but I glanced downstream and saw my two-year old's little plaid shorts several feet away. At that moment, I realized he was floating face down in the water. I ran through the water, reaching him as quickly as I could, and when I lifted him up out of the water, he didn't cry. He just looked at me. He must have been holding his breath under water because he was fine. Praise God, I was able to save him. Had he not been wearing those brightly colored shorts, I don't think I would have seen him. I shudder to think the current would have taken him away. We would have lost him,

but I know that wasn't God's plan.  He
protected him.

I Kept These As A Reminder Of God's Protection

## A Hard Kick

Our eight-year old daughter was kicked
by a Clydesdale horse and knocked to the
ground while we were watching a parade.  I
rode with her in the ambulance to the
hospital.  I remember praying over her and
telling her God was with us and He was
taking care of her.  She had x-rays which
revealed that the horse's hoof had just
missed her kidney.  The doctor wanted her to
spend the night in the hospital for
observation, but when I told him I was a

nurse, he let us bring her home. Her dad and I prayed over her, and I checked her vital signs and watched for any signs of internal bleeding, then finally went to bed. The doctor had said she would have severe bruising and it would be painful for her to walk, but she danced into our room early the next morning and said, "I don't even hurt." And what was totally amazing was she never had any bruising. Medically, it could not be explained, but God!

## The Bill

One December, not long before Christmas, and at a time when Al was out of work, we had a large, unexpected car repair bill. As Al left to pick up the car from the repair shop, I walked out to get the mail. There was an envelope from the gas and electric company. Inside was a letter explaining they owed us money, along with a check. When Al returned, he was so down as he told me the cost of the repair. I then showed him the check we had received, and it was for exactly $100 less than the car repair bill. We had never received a refund from the utility company before, nor have we ever since!  I then heard the Lord's voice tell me we were going to receive $100, and it would be in a way we least expected.  I told that to Al, but we shared it with no one else.

Three days later, he returned from his men's group meeting at church with a large manila envelope, along with instructions for us to open it together.  There was an award certificate and note from a family in our church, stating they had chosen us to receive the Inspiration Award from their family that year.  The note explained that they presented this award each year to the person or family that had most inspired them that year.  And clipped to the certificate was a check for $100!  God had told me we would be getting that money and that we would not expect to get it in the way we did!

## Blocked Surgery

I had routine blood work done, and one of the levels that could indicate ovarian cancer was too high.  I was scheduled for exploratory surgery.  I was in pre-op when the anesthesiologist came in to check me.

She said, "You can't have surgery. You have bronchitis." I had no symptoms of bronchitis, but my surgery was rescheduled. I returned to the hospital on the rescheduled day, and once again, the anesthesiologist came in to check me, and once again, I heard those same words, "You can't have surgery. You have bronchitis." And, again, I had no symptoms. So home I went a second time! Throughout my life, I have struggled with fear, but only about health and safety issues. Since Satan always attacks our weakest areas, those have been the most difficult for me to entrust to the Lord. But when I was sent home the second time, I believed He was telling me to trust Him completely. I really believe He was protecting me from unnecessary surgery. I never did have it, and that was thirty years ago! Of course, surgery is often necessary, and I'm not advocating going against one's doctor. I am just saying we need to listen to God.

## Tithe

Over thirty years ago, we knew God was calling us to tithe. Al and I had been praying about it, and we discussed it over our morning coffee one day. We made the decision to tithe, but we were concerned about the amount we would have to increase our giving. In the mail that very same day was our confirmation from the Lord. There was a check we weren't expecting, and it was for $1.30 more than the amount we needed to increase our giving. That check was already in the mail before we had even made our decision or figured out the amount. Once we made that decision to tithe, we have always done so, no matter what our financial situation has been. God has always provided for us, and I can say, without hesitation, you can never out-give God!

## $1,000 Prize

I love to take pictures! Last year, I entered a very unique photo in a contest in a magazine. The top prize was $1000. Several people had seen my photo and commented that they thought it was a prize-winner. Soon after entering the contest, I was in church. There was a young man there who, during the Prayer and Praise time of the service, shared that he needed prayer because his car had broken down. He had no money to get it repaired and no way to get to work. As a result, he had lost his job. While sitting there, a thought came to me that I would give him $100 if I won the $1,000. It was then that I heard that voice in my spirit say "No, don't give it if you win. Give it now." My immediate thought was, "Wow, if I obey God and give the $100 now, I think He is going to bless me by having me win the $1000."

A few minutes later, during our pastor's message, he spoke about giving, which is something he never did. He said God blesses us when we give from our hearts. He said God's blessings come in many forms and we should never give with our motive being to be blessed as a result. He then went on, saying, "For example, we should never give $100 expecting to get $1,000 in return." My mouth fell open, and I gasped audibly. Talk about God speaking! I was blown away! I did give the $100 in obedience to the Lord. By the way, I didn't win a thing in the contest!

# God's Hand on Our Son

Our youngest son is a gifted musician who plays the piano. When he was eight years old, he wrote a song entitled The King's Symphony, and he said it was a love song to Jesus. He played it in the County Fair talent show. He won first place and went on to the State Fair where he won first place in the state semi-finals, then 4th place in the Grand Championship finals.

Molly, the lady who was in charge of the dressing rooms, took me aside the first day we were there and said,"God has His hand on that boy!" I asked why she said that, and her response was, "God told me to tell you that." She didn't know we were Christians, and that was before she even knew what he would be playing! No one is too young to bring glory to God!

While he was in college, he spent some time in Puerto Rico, touring with a big band. Late one night, after Al and I were already in bed, he called and said they were in a very dangerous city and they were told not to venture out alone during the day and not at all at night.  Upon hearing this, I became anxious and afraid.  Of course, I told him his dad and I would pray for his safety.  We hung up, and Al and I prayed.  It was then that the Lord gave me a vision of my son walking on a sidewalk with an angel walking ahead of him, an angel walking behind him and one on each side of him.

We read in Psalm 91:11 (NIV), " For He will command His angels concerning you, to guard you in all your ways."  What a promise!  I closed my eyes and fell asleep, completely at peace, and our son was safe!

Recently, I was telling my twelve year old grandson about the vision I had when his dad was in Puerto Rico.  His response was, "What about on the diagonal?"  The only angels I "saw" were the ones I described, but I'm sure the Lord had the diagonal covered as well!

## Funeral Song

Sometimes Al and I used to sing a hymn together when we were in the car.  It was, "What a Day That Will Be" by Jim Hill.  I guess Al must have mentioned it to a friend once. Now, he never sang in school. I was in chorus in school, but I am definitely not a singer! Well, our friend's wife passed away, and he told Al he wanted him and me to sing that hymn at his wife's funeral. Al told him we weren't singers and that we had <u>never</u> done anything like that before. Our friend said he didn't care, he still wanted us to sing it at the funeral. So, we prayed hard, really hard, and we practiced it a couple of times with our pastor's wife accompanying us on the piano.

The day arrived, the service began, and soon we were up on the altar singing our duet, our knees knocking. At the end of the funeral, three or four people complimented us, and one woman even asked where we usually sang. When I told her we didn't sing anywhere and we had never sung before, her response was, "Oh, that was so beautiful. I thought you were professionals!" Don't ever doubt the presence of the Holy Spirit and His involvement in your life. He sang through us that day, and that is what the people heard!

# Scripture: The Key to Peace

God often uses Scripture to speak to His children, and I have experienced that. I had to have a cardiac ultrasound, and it showed something abnormal, so it had to be followed up with an angiogram. I was anxious upon hearing that something might be wrong with my heart. The devotional I was reading from ended two days before the scheduled angiogram, and the entry for that day was on Philippians 4:7 (NIV), "And the peace of God, which transcends all understanding, will guard your hearts and your minds in Christ Jesus." I picked out a new devotional to use, and the entry for that next day was also Philippians 4:7. I turned on the TV that morning and watched Charles Stanley. At the end of the program, he quoted Philippians 4:6 (NIV), "Do not be anxious about anything, but in everything, by prayer and petition, with thanksgiving, present your requests to God." All three of those things were confirmation to me from God himself that He was in control. I didn't need to be anxious. He told me He was guarding my heart! I had total peace as I had the angiogram, everything was normal,

and I had another experience to add to my
long list of evidences of God's faithfulness.

## How Many Fingers?

For so many years, Al had traveled as he
worked in the construction field. One night,
I was sound asleep, and he woke me up
saying he could see out of his "bad" eye. He
was covering his good eye with his hand as
he told me. He had eye surgery as a child,
and something went wrong, and he had lost
most of his eyesight in his right eye. I
doubted if he really was seeing, thinking
maybe he was talking in his sleep. So, I
held up two fingers and asked how many
fingers he saw, and when he answered
correctly, I held up four, and again, he gave
the correct answer. God had healed his
eyesight!

When he went in to work the following
Monday, he was promoted to management.
That involved much preparing and reading
of reports and blueprints in the local office.
Had he not regained his eyesight, he would
have been unable to carry out that job,
because he used to get severe eyestrain if he

read for too long.  Was this God's timing intersecting with His purposes?  We praised God because he would no longer be traveling for work.

## His Shield

Psalm 28:7 (NIV) says,
"The Lord is my strength and shield.
My heart trusts in Him, and I am helped."

Psalm 46:1 (NIV) tells us, "
God is our refuge and strength,
an ever- present help in trouble."

I have prayed for the Lord's protection for my family for years.  One day, Al was driving our car, and I was in the passenger seat.  I glanced out my side window and saw a deer bounding through the field.  I think I thought she would stop at the road and wait for traffic (duh!), but she smashed through my window.  At that moment, an invisible shield seemed to come between us, and the deer's head hit it, missing my head by literally an inch!  My husband was very concerned and asked if I was okay.  I was fine. My only "injury" was a tiny cut on my finger that had been hit by a sliver of glass.

I was amazed at what had just happened. I couldn't believe the deer's head hit something solid that didn't appear to be there. It was then that I heard the Lord speak in my spirit. He said, "You always pray for a protective shield. Why would you be surprised that I would give you one?"

## Barren No More

Our daughter was unable to have children. We were all pretty devastated. Many of us prayed that God would bless her with a baby. Her youngest brother and his wife already had a baby, and then her other brother and sister-in-law told her just before their dad's birthday that they were expecting. They told her they were going to tell us at Al's birthday gathering. That was so thoughtful of them. They knew that was going to be so difficult for her. She called us the day of the birthday party and said she and her husband would not be coming. I was disappointed and told her so. I wanted everyone to be there and for the day to be special for her dad. Her response was, "Oh, it will be special." When I found out about the upcoming arrival of another baby in our family, of course I was overjoyed, but I then knew why she couldn't be there. It was too painful for her.

After several years of disappointment and the bittersweet realization of seeing both of her younger brothers become dads, a miracle finally happened. It was Mothers' Day, and she and her husband gave me my gift. I unwrapped it, and it was a framed picture of an ultrasound. Her brother and his wife had just had a baby girl the previous month, and as I looked at the picture, I was puzzled and thought, "Why are they giving me a framed picture of our new granddaughter's ultrasound?" It took a couple of minutes for it to register that they were expecting and that was their baby. We were all overjoyed!

A few months after her son was born and while she was still nursing him, she called me one day, saying she was so exhausted and nauseated. She thought she had the flu. I asked if she could be pregnant, and her answer was a definite "no." She reiterated what a hard time she had getting pregnant the first time, and she also reminded me that she was nursing the baby.

My son-in-law had taken several wonderful pictures of the baby, and I asked for copies of a few of them. They brought them over a couple of weeks later. As I was thumbing through them, I came to one of him sitting in his bumbo seat, and my daughter's hand was holding a sign in front of him that said, "I'm going to be a big brother." Wow! God is so good! Our granddaughter was born on my birthday! When she was almost four years old, I asked her what happened on March 19. "I was born, and you got the present," was her response. What a double blessing to go to our daughter's home and see not one, but two nurseries and two cribs and see her pushing a double stroller!

## Health Concerns

One of my grandsons had a hemangioma on his eyelid that began to grow very rapidly after he was about a month old. His parents took him to the doctor, and they were told there was a chance he might lose his eyesight in that eye. Of course, we prayed!

One Sunday in church during that time, we sang the song, *"He Knows My Name."* How that ministered to me, reminding me that He had created the baby, and He was in control of all that was happening.

Not long after that, another of our grandsons had to have an EEG following what was thought to be a petit mal (mini) seizure. I had the radio on in the car the day of his test, and that same song came on. Once again, God used it to minister to me, to enable me to rest in Him! By age two, my one grandson's hemangioma was virtually gone on its own, and the EEG showed no abnormalities, and that grandson has been fine.

## Our New Home

We have lived in our current home for ten years. When we put our previous house on the market, the realtor told us what she thought we should list it for, but we felt we could get more, so we listed it for $20,000 more than she recommended. We then began our search for our new home, but after seeing many, none had been what we wanted. Finally, the realtor told us we could never get the house we were looking for at the price we were willing to pay. We reluctantly agreed to look at some more expensive homes. She then took us to see two houses. We really didn't care for the first one, but as we were leaving it, there was a rainbow in the sky, and it was arched right over the area where the second house was located. We got there, and the moment we walked in the door, we both knew we had found our house. Al had seen it online but had never considered it because it was way above our price range. However, the sellers had just lowered the price by $35,000! It was still priced a little higher than our budget, but we put in an offer, and it was accepted. We did make it contingent on us selling our house.

Time went by, and we had no offers on our house, which had four bedrooms, two full baths and two thousand square feet, perfect for a family. Several families looked at it, but no offers came in. One hot day in

July, a widow in her 70s came with her realtor. Al and I usually left when the house was being shown, but that evening, we sat out in the yard. She spent about ten minutes in the house, walked once around the yard and left. "So much for that," we thought. Several days later, we received a call from our realtor, telling us that the sellers of the house on which we had the offer were willing to drop the already accepted price by $10,000 if we would be willing to remove the contingency. That was definitely scary since we still had no offer on our house, but we said a quick prayer and decided to do it. One hour later, we received another call. That one was the realtor telling us there was an offer on our house, and it was the single woman who had quickly walked through it that one time. And, her offer was for only $5000 less than our asking price. We ended up getting our current home for just $10.000 more than we had budgeted to spend, but ended up selling our house for $15,000 more than the realtor told us we could get. That left us $5000 ahead.

After we got moved into our new home, we decided to add a sunroom . We obtained a couple of estimates from builders in the area, but they were quite high. One day, I was driving down the road in town, and I stopped for a red light. A pick-up truck pulled up in the lane beside me. It was another local builder. I copied the phone number printed on the side of the truck and called him. He gave us an estimate, and it was for $3500 less than the lowest of the other two estimates. We hired him to build our sunroom, and it's exactly what we wanted.

## Cancer

Al had a routine stress test, and it went well. However, on the physical exam, the doctor felt a small aortic aneurysm. He said it needed to be watched. A few months later, it was checked and it had not grown. However, he had a mass in his kidney. Had he not had the aneurysm, the mass may not have been found until it was too late. God allowed it to be found before he had any symptoms, and later, the aneurysm could not be found. He had surgery. The surgeon removed both the mass and a portion of his kidney. The report came back the following week, and it showed that the mass was malignant.

Two days after finding out that Al had cancer, our daughter, Theresa was diagnosed with Hodgkin's Lymphoma. My heart felt as if it was breaking upon getting that news, and my fears surfaced. Although we prayed and many others were praying, there were moments I thought that I might lose both my husband and my daughter. I had to get to the point where I was able to give them to the Lord. It was truly an Abraham experience! I thought of him taking his son, Isaac up the mountain and being willing to sacrifice him. I was not nearly as obedient as he was. I wrestled long and hard, crying out to God in anguish before being able to take that step.

Theresa had surgery the week after Al had his surgery. He was home with a drain, and I wouldn't leave him alone, yet I wanted to be at the hospital with our son-in-law as Theresa had her surgery. God calls us to be there for each other, and our friends certainly were there for us. Dear friends came and stayed with Al so I could go to the hospital. And two of my closest friends came and sat with us at the hospital. The surgery took longer than expected, and I began to get really anxious. They prayed with me as one sat on either side of me. I am not Moses, but they were definitely my Aaron and Hur!

Al recovered from his surgery. Theresa had chemo and radiation with her husband by her side while I took care of their two pre-schoolers. When it was time for her chemo treatments every other week, I would get anxious and not feel well. I stayed with her and the kids the day after each chemo session. One day, when she came out of the bathroom after getting ill from the chemo, I began to cry. Her faith was strong, and SHE comforted ME, telling me it was okay. The only response I was able to give was, "It's not okay." It broke my heart to see her suffer. How our Heavenly Father must grieve over us just as we grieve over our children!

This was a very difficult time in all of our lives, but we did feel God's presence through it all. Lysa Terkeurst says, "Weak moments don't make weak faith. Weak moments make us even more aware of our need to press in to faith," and "Every time we face anything that causes us to cry out to God, let's declare that this hard time will be a holy time, a close-to-God time."

Sometimes our journey is really hard and painful, and we are weak, but all God requires of us at those times is for us to take His hand and lean on Him for the strength we need. And, as I've heard it said, without the test, there would be no testimony. God doesn't waste anything we go through.

One day, while Theresa was going through chemotherapy, I wanted to put a picture of her in my Bible, not that I needed it there to remind me to pray for her. The Bible, which has very small print, was on the coffee table and was facing the couch, so from where I was standing, the print was upside down. I opened it, and one line literally popped out, in large print, and it was "nor shall I know the loss of children." I put on my glasses because I can't read without them, and I read the entire passage. It was Isaiah 47:8 (NKJV), and the line above the one that had popped out was "I shall not sit as a widow." The rest of the passage did not pertain, but once again, God used Scripture to speak to me with those few words. When something literally jumps off the page in the Bible, we know, without a doubt, that is God speaking to us.

Theresa And Her Children During Her Chemo Treatments

Even though they both still had tests, treatments and bad days to face, and the cancer didn't just miraculously go away, those words of Scripture comforted me and filled me with His peace. I am reminded of the quote by Leslie Gould, "Sometimes God calms the storm, and sometimes God lets the storm rage and calms His child."

I know there are those who have lost spouses or children who are reading this right now. I don't understand why mine survived while some others haven't, but I do know that God knows best in each of our situations. He has the perfect plan and sees the whole picture while we see only parts of it. God spared my husband's and daughter's lives! All praise and glory to Him!

It has been over seven years, and our daughter is cancer-free. Al survived the kidney cancer, but two years ago, he was diagnosed with a new cancer, unrelated to the initial one. He had surgery for that, and so far, all is well. Throughout all of these years, we have known that God is in complete control of our lives, and our trials have caused our faith and trust in Him to grow.

## Built on the Rock

For our 45th anniversary, Al and I renewed our vows on the shore of the Atlantic Ocean. As he gave me a beautiful blue opal ring, he told me he chose that specific ring because the jeweler told him if an opal is blue, it means it has grown on a rock. He knew he had to get it for me

Renewing our vows on the ocean shore on our 45th anniversary

because he said our marriage has been built on the Rock, Jesus Christ.

Soon after that, Al had a doctor appointment. He was in the chair in the examination room when he saw a photograph on the wall of a brook with a rock in it, and on the rock was a blue stone that appeared to be growing on it. He was so excited when he came home and told me. The Lord really blessed both of us!

Speaking of Jesus, the Rock, I was down by the water one day when I saw a heron standing on a rock in the water. I watched him for some time. The water was splashing up on the rock, but the heron never moved. I received a clear message from the Lord that day. We need to always stand on the Rock, no matter how strong the waves are crashing around us, no matter our circumstances. We need to build on Jesus, the Rock.

In Isaiah 26:4 (NIV), we read, "Trust in the Lord forever, for the Lord, the Lord is the Rock eternal." As the song, "The Solid Rock" by Edward Mote says, "On Christ the solid rock I stand, all other ground is sinking sand… When all around my soul gives way, He then is all my hope and stay."

Our faith in Him and our trust in Him together form the solid foundation that helps us to weather the storms in our lives. Peter walked on water, but only while he had his eyes on his Lord. When he took his eyes off of Jesus and looked around and saw the huge waves that were all around him, he began to sink. When we go through tough times, we need to keep our eyes on Jesus and not on our circumstances or we will sink.

# Chapter 4

# God in the Little Things

## The Perfect Rose

Our Heavenly Father cares about the big important details of our lives, but does He care about the smallest ones as well?  I know He truly does!  Since Al worked in construction, it was not unusual for him to be out of work.  At those times, we were very careful with our spending, buying only what was essential.  One year, on our anniversary, I got up that morning, and there in a vase on the table was an absolutely exquisite dew-kissed rose.  Al had noticed one closed bud on a bush in the yard about two weeks before.  He checked on it every day, praying each day that it would not open until our anniversary the first week in October. We have never seen a rose growing in October before. It is highly unusual where we live in Upstate New York. When he went out the morning of our anniversary, it was perfect! God answered his prayer, and I was so blessed by the beautiful expression of my husband's love for me, by God's provision and by the awesome beauty of His creation!

## Lobster

One anniversary several years ago, Al and I went out to a seafood restaurant for dinner. I wanted a rock lobster tail so badly, but it was so expensive, I ordered something else. Al ordered a shrimp dish, but by mistake, the waiter brought him a rock lobster tail. When Al said that wasn't what he ordered, the waiter said it was their mistake, so there would be no charge for it. Since Al doesn't love lobster, he gave it to me, and the waiter brought the meal he had ordered. Psalm 37:4 (NIV) says, "Delight yourself in the Lord, and He will give you the desires of your heart." He knew the desire of my heart, and He also knew that I was trying to be a good steward. That lobster was God's gift to me!

## Our Dog, D.J.

We had a beautiful black lab. One day, she ran away. She was gone all night. We prayed for her to come home. We drove all around town looking for her. As I was driving, I prayed for a sign that she was okay. We went to the park, and there was only one other car there, and on the bumper was a sticker that read "Awesome God." That really was all the encouragement I needed, and I took it as the sign from God. I had the Christian radio station on, and right after I saw the sticker, the speaker talked about a dog. We didn't find her as we drove around, but when we went home, the phone was ringing. It was a police officer telling us that our dog was at the police department.

## The President

All three of my kids were in the fife and drum corps. Ronald Reagan was president at that time and was coming to our nearest city.  The fife and drum corps got selected to play for him as he disembarked from his plane, Air Force One.  I went with the group as one of the chaperones, and of course, I had my camera to capture the moment.  When we arrived at the airport, the group was taken into a room and searched and wanded.  Somehow, I guess it was assumed that I was an "official" photographer, so I was given a special sticker and allowed out on the tarmac along with the group.  President Reagan walked right over to the kids and spoke to them.  I was able to get some really good pictures.  That was such a special experience for the kids.

Picture I took of President Reagan as our kids performed for him

I was especially blessed because I really admired our president for his faith in God and his values!

## The Blessing of Tree Peonies

A friend gave me a beautiful tree peony blossom, and I put it in a vase, hoping it would still be beautiful two days later. I would be entertaining eight ladies at a formal tea in my home, and the dinner plate-sized peony would make the perfect centerpiece. However, the morning of the tea, several of the petals had fallen off, so I wasn't able to use it. I wanted to call my friend and ask for another one, but I was reluctant to do so, thinking it rather presumptuous. At that moment, as I was hesitating, the phone rang. It was that friend. She said she and her husband were going to be out of town for a few days, and her tree peonies were all in full bloom. She told me to feel free to go pick some from her yard. I picked three, and they made a gorgeous centerpiece on my table!

## Not Ready

Twelve years ago, I had a dream. It was a very spiritual dream! I was getting married, and I was in my gown at the church. All of the guests were there, and I realized I did not have my veil. I had previously studied about our wedding dress being our character and how getting our wedding dress ready meant becoming more Christ-like as we get ready for the day we meet our Bridegroom. The fact that I didn't have my veil indicated to me that I wasn't ready to meet Him. There were still areas in my life that needed to be conformed into His image. I pray that I am more like Him today than I was then and that others see Him in me and desire a closer relationship with Him because of their contact with me.

## God's Concern

I got up in the night one night, and I didn't turn on a light. I smashed into the door frame. An x-ray showed I had cracked a rib. The next morning's devotional in Sarah Young's *Jesus Calling* started out with "I am the God who heals. I heal broken bodies." What a personal God! He knew exactly what I was going through, and He showed He cared.

## A Special Treat

We have a cottage an hour away from our home, and we like to go there once in a while for a day or two to get away. One day, we drove there, and just before arriving, we realized we had forgotten the coffee. Well, my husband cannot live without his coffee, and I do enjoy a cup each morning. However, the distance round trip to the nearest grocery store is fourteen miles. Just as we pulled in the driveway, our neighbor came to the car and handed us a bag. In it was a pound of special coffee that we really enjoy, but we don't buy because it's too expensive for every day use. Not only did God have it all under control, He provided us with the best!

## Tea Party Delivery

I called a friend one day, and she was very discouraged. She had fallen a week before and had injured her ankle. She was in a lot of pain and needed to be off her foot. After we hung up, God led me to pack a tea party in a basket. I packed bone china tea cups and plates, linen napkins, cookies, a small bouquet of flowers, everything needed for a tea. I took it to her, and that, along with my visit, was just what she needed.

When we feel a "nudge" from the Lord, we need to listen and follow up on it. In Ephesians 6, verse 7 (NIV), we are told to "serve wholeheartedly, as if you were serving the Lord, not men…" God will use us in big and small ways when our purpose in life is to serve Him and bless others. In the process of serving, we too will be blessed!

## Polly Pockets

I was online one day and saw some cute little dolls called Polly Pockets. I ordered them. I have four young granddaughters, and none of them had ever mentioned them, but I ordered them anyway. The week after they arrived in the mail, I was at Community Bible Study, and one of the ladies shared that she was part of a team going on a mission trip. They needed some toys. She mentioned one specific toy for boys and Polly Pocket dolls for girls! I was so excited to be able to donate the ones I ordered because I saw it as one more thing orchestrated by the Lord! That really spoke to me that absolutely nothing is insignificant to God.

If we would take the time to look back over our lives, every one of us would be able to see God at work. The same God who spoke to and worked in the lives of the men and women of the Bible is the same God who orchestrates everything in our lives today. In all four gospels, we read of Jesus feeding 5000 with five loaves of bread and two fish. On another occasion, shortly after having seen that the very large crowd had been fed and that there were even 12 baskets of leftovers, the disciples still were not sure how the crowd of 4000 that had gathered would be fed. Didn't they remember how Jesus multiplied the little they had before so it was more than enough to feed everyone? They had seen it with their own eyes, yet they were doubtful that He could or would do it again. Aren't we the same way? God proves to us that He is faithful in our lives, yet when "the next thing" comes along, we doubt that He will come through for us. We need to recall all of the times He has cared for us in the past and trust Him to be faithful again. Meditate on Psalm 100:5 (NIV), "For the Lord is good and His love endures forever; His faithfulness continues through all generations."

# Chapter 5

# His Hands, Our Hearts, Their Feet

It was 4:00 AM Christmas Eve. The gifts were piled to the ceiling in the kitchen and spilling into the living room. All thirteen drivers would be arriving in less than four hours to help deliver them. As we looked around at the brightly colored wrapped gifts before going to flop into bed for a couple of hours, Al and I both sensed the presence of the Lord. What had started out five years before with us helping one family had mushroomed into the Caring Center, an organization of many bringing Christmas to 137 families. Through all the growth, we knew that this was truly the Lord's project. We were His hands!

How well I remember that first Christmas we decided to share with another family. Al had been laid off the previous year, so we weren't able to do much for our family for Christmas. None of us felt deprived though. We had two young children, and I made new pajamas for them. Al made a doll house for our daughter, while I made furniture for it from empty cartons covered with contact paper. He also made a wooden truck for our son. It really was probably one of our best Christmases since our focus was on the true meaning of the holiday, and we were able to spend precious time together! As a result of that year, we decided to provide Christmas for a family in need.

With Christmas approaching, we read in our church bulletin about a woman and her three children who needed housing. We could not offer them housing, but we knew we could at least make Christmas a little brighter for them. I called the church for information and stated that we wanted to provide Christmas for them. The receptionist gave me their names and ages, along with their address.

I told a friend about them, and we made a list of things we wanted to buy for them. Then, we went on a shopping spree. We had a great time making our selections - a pretty dress and a doll for the little girl, a big truck for one of the boys, a set of building blocks for the other one, pajamas for all of them, and finally, socks for all three of them. We purchased a scarf and mitten set for the mom. We also fixed a fruit basket and put it under the tree along with the other gifts.

Al and I invited them to our home for Christmas dinner. The mother didn't drive, so he went to pick them up. It was a cold, snowy day, as are most of our Christmases in Upstate New York. They arrived wearing sweaters, but no coats. No one was wearing boots. The children wore sneakers with NO SOCKS! And we had new socks for each of them!

"Lord, it is such a good feeling to dress our children in nice warm pajamas on cold winter nights and in warm, furry coats, mittens, fuzzy-lined boots and knit caps to go out into the blustery cold. Help us to not be oblivious to the fact that there are children in our own town who don't even own socks," I prayed. From the moment we saw those little bare feet, our lives would never, could never, be the same. They all put their socks on as soon as they unwrapped them, and we put their sneakers on registers to dry.

We had a truly beautiful birthday for Jesus, and we knew then that somehow, we would always be sharing our Christmases with others less fortunate than ourselves. Our two children were just six and four, but they too sensed something very special about that Christmas.

A lot of changes took place in our lives the following year. We were expecting our third child. One day while visiting some friends in the country, we saw a big, old farmhouse that was for sale. We stopped to look at it, and it was love at first sight. "It needs work, but we love challenges, right?" Al said, as he looked at me with a look that told me his mind was already made up. As we went through it, my mind was racing. What would we ever do with all that room? The rooms were huge!

What really sold us, though, was that just as we were leaving with the realtor, the sun was setting behind two churches just down the road. Al and I looked at each other, and we knew that this was where the Lord wanted us. We got the house and began remodeling it. Our third child, another son, was born, and we moved in one month later.

By Christmas of that year, we were completely settled and wanted to help a family again. We heard about a family of ten who was to have a meager Christmas. They were Christians, so they would know the joy of celebrating the birthday of the Son of God, but as we looked at our own children and thought of the disappointment of those eight little ones when they found nothing under their tree on Christmas morning, we knew we were to help them. My friend helped again, and what fun we had gathering up just the right gift for each of them. When our kids each picked out one of their own toys to give to them, our joy was even more complete.

We delivered the gifts on Christmas Eve. No one was home, so we left them in an abandoned car in the driveway. Just before leaving, we hung a fresh pine wreath on an old fencepost in the front yard. Later, we learned that while the man was at work, he found out that one of his co-workers had just lost everything in a fire. While driving home, he was trying to think of some way he could help that family. When he arrived home, his children showed him everything we had dropped off. He told them about the fire, and they all sat down and divided up everything they had received, and they shared with the family who had the fire. What a joy to find out that through our efforts, a family who might otherwise have had nothing to give was able to help someone worse off than themselves. We enabled then to be Christ to another family!

The new year arrived, and we approached it with the satisfaction that we had given of ourselves to make someone else happy. It was a good feeling. We had thoughts of doing the same thing the following Christmas. Little did we know then what the Lord had in mind! The following Christmas was coming. We planned on helping the same family, and we decided to expand our ministry to include two families. We tried to find another needy family.

Less than a week before Christmas, we heard of a family who had been evicted from their home. The husband and wife were despondent, and both had contemplated suicide. They had two small children. We began our search for them, but we were unsuccessful at first. In the process of trying to locate them, though, we heard about nine other families who could use help. We really had a lot of work to do to gather enough gifts for ten families. This was really growing into something big.

Off to the store we marched to stock up on socks, toys and games for the children and lotion and after shave for the adults. Christmas Eve arrived, and we made it. We were ready. Our daughter came down the stairs, looked at the piles of gifts all over the kitchen and exclaimed, "This looks like a caring center.!" From that moment on, we became known as the Caring Center. It was never our intention to give a care package to anyone, but rather, we put a lot of thought and effort into making sure the gifts were special for each person. We gave "caring" packages!

People began to hear what we were doing. Someone donated jewelry appropriate for teen girls. The local Christian school donated two trees. Four of us moms got together in my kitchen that morning and wrapped and tagged everything. Our children, ten in all, were in the living room stringing popcorn and making construction paper ornaments for the two trees. Al went to pick up the trees.

While he was gone, the phone rang. It was a friend who knew of a woman and her two teen girls who had nothing. "Great," I thought, "we have the jewelry." Then he told me they didn't even have a tree. "Tree? We have a tree!" I exclaimed. I think that was the beginning of our realization that

Jesus Himself was in our kitchen directing the entire effort. He was supplying every need before we even realized the need was there!

When Al returned from getting the trees, he was carrying three pair of girls' knee socks. Someone had put them on the dashboard of his truck. He could not find out how they got there. Not too many people knew what we were doing at that point, but I had a strong feeling the Lord put them there so we would try again to locate the despondent family. After several phone calls, I found out they were staying in a local motel. They had a girl, six and a boy, eight. I asked the desk clerk if they were in need, and her response was, "Are they ever!" I told her we would take care of their Christmas. Needless to say, the little girl received the knee socks!

We shivered in the cold, piercing wind as we loaded everything into cars and started on our way. Our first stop was the home of the family of ten we had helped the previous year. Our intention was to drop the packages at the door and run, but the man saw us and insisted we come in. The family was seated around the table eating lunch, and the kitchen was not very large. There were fourteen of us, four adults and ten children, and we made a circle behind them around the table. The father suggested we all sing, "Away in a Manger." What a glorious, emotional few minutes! Through our tears, we could see the beautiful little faces of our children in their colorful snowsuits with the fur around their rosy cheeks blending in with the beautiful little faces of their children in their worn, faded clothing, and instantly, we felt that bond of being brothers and sisters in Christ. How much the Lord, and that family, gave us in those few short minutes! However, that was just the beginning of the many "gifts" we were to receive that day.

We continued on our merry way, feeling like we were being transported on a cloud. We were on a real high, and with each stop, we seemed to get higher. At one house, an elderly woman who lived alone came to the door. I handed her a package and wished her a Merry Christmas. She asked who it was from, and I just told her it was from some friends.  She looked at me with the sweetest expression, gave a sigh and embraced me.  I remember thinking, "This has got to stop.  I'll never make it."  We left packages on porches or just inside doors of places where people were not home.  We took turns running to the doors, and we hurried to try to avoid being asked too many questions.

A few stops later, we were at a trailer, and it was my turn again, so I went to the door and knocked.  No one answered.  I could see that a lamp was on.  I tried the door, thinking I would just set the box inside.  The door was unlocked, and I saw a small Christmas tree at the other end of the room.  I tiptoed in and spread all the gifts under the tree and left with the big empty box under my arm.  I felt like Santa Claus!  Imagine that family's surprise when they got home or maybe even came out of another room!

We were almost finished - just two stops left.  The next family was a woman and her four young boys.  We pulled into the driveway, and all four of them came running out, barefooted and bare chested!  It was a bitter, cold, rainy day. Again, we had new socks for all of the boys. At least their feet would be warm. We had some new toys for each of them, as well. We felt good.

We were sure they were the family who would need the second tree we had been carrying all along, since our final stop would be the motel. We were sure they couldn't have a full-size, live tree in a motel room, and at that point, we also knew that the Lord would not have provided the tree unless someone needed it. Could we be wrong about that? They already had a tree, so we would be taking it back with us.

On we went to the motel. We would leave the gifts at the main desk. The man there said he thought it would be nice if we ALL went down to the room and delivered them ourselves. At that moment, I thought we had nothing to lose, so I told him about the full-size tree and reluctantly asked if they could have it. His reply was, "Sure, I even have a stand they can use. Just ask them to return it when they are finished with it." Amazing! The Lord did have it all planned out! Why had we had doubts?

We were so excited and enthusiastic at that point. We were totally unprepared for the scene that awaited us behind that door. All fourteen of us were standing there with the tree, the stand, the box of ornaments our children had made, and the gifts. Wouldn't they be surprised? One of us knocked. The boy opened the door, and he was in his underwear. He was embarrassed and ran in to the bathroom. The man and the little girl were not there. The woman was lying on one of the beds, and she had to weigh well over 300 pounds. She was dirty and seemed lethargic. She made no effort to get up or even to acknowledge our presence. How ungrateful! The drapes were drawn, and it was real dreary and smelly. And here we were, so full of the wonder and the excitement of the birth of Jesus! I was, I am ashamed to say, repulsed by the whole scene and just wanted to get out of there quickly.

I glanced at a small mirror on the wall, and there was a lone piece of silver garland, about eighteen inches long, draped from one corner of the mirror to the other. That was the only sign of Christmas in the whole room. We put the tree in the stand, and someone set the box of homemade ornaments next to it. After putting some packages on the floor, I straightened up, only to see the woman standing right in front of me, tears trickling down her cheeks. At that moment, I saw Jesus Christ more clearly than I had ever seen Him before, and I embraced that woman. I know the Lord heard the prayer in my heart, "Oh, God, forgive me for judging. Forgive me for the feelings I had toward this woman, Your precious child. From this moment on, help me to see everyone as the unique person made in Your image. Help me to look beyond the external and see Christ in him or her."

We drove home less bubbly, but definitely warmed by the experience of Christ being in our midst. Our son, who was five at the time, broke the silence with, "twelve families this year, maybe next year, we can help twenty-five." So that became our goal for the following year. We were into this in a big way now, and we were absolutely positive that the Lord would not only provide the families, but also the means to bring Christmas to each and every one of them.

As I said earlier, we were unaware at the beginning of that day of all the gifts the Lord intended to shower upon us on that very special day, the eve before His birthday. As I sat in church that night, I couldn't help feeling we had already had Christmas. What a celebration we had for Him, and He made us feel like the guests of honor!

The following year, we did not share with twenty-five families. Instead, we had sixty! We had volunteer drivers at that point and divided the territory we had to cover into five routes. That year, we also began making up packages of baked goods and handmade cards made by children in art class in school for the inmates in the county jail. The principal of the parochial school in town allowed me to go in to the eighth grade class, and we made homemade candy for the families. Some local stores began donating toys. There were again many remarkable moments. However, two will always stand out in my mind.

We had everything we needed for all of the people, but we were short one gift for a little four year old girl. We needn't have been concerned. A friend brought over a small table-top piano and said she thought we might be able to use it. This may sound strange, but each year as we put packages together, I picked out certain dolls, trucks or games, toys that I felt would be just right for each particular child, even though I didn't know them. I'm sure it wouldn't have mattered to them, but somehow, I felt that we had a special gift for each one. Since the piano was all we had to give that little girl, we had no choice. Maybe she would rather have had something else.

When we arrived at her house, no one was home. The doors were locked, and there was no porch. The only place we could put gifts was in the mailbox. I opened the mailbox and slid the wrapped piano into it. It fit perfectly without an inch to spare. I knew then that little piano was the perfect gift for that little girl. I wouldn't be surprised if she had asked Santa for a piano!

There was another very special happening that year. We took some extra fresh fruit and homemade Christmas cookies and candies with us on our deliveries. We had an address for one Spanish family, but we couldn't locate them. Supposedly, they lived in an apartment building on a very short street, but we didn't have the apartment number. We knocked on one door, and the man who came to the door didn't know the people, but he tried to help us. Before long, people were coming out of their apartments to see what was going on, and several tried to help. Small children peered out of windows to see who had come into their little neighborhood. No one spoke English, and we spoke no Spanish. What a time we had trying to communicate!

We never did find that family, but we passed out all of the goodies we had to those people. We didn't understand each others' language, but we understood their kindness and helpfulness, and they understood our appreciation. Even though the air on that December 24th was cold and crisp, our hearts were warmed by the bond that was created between our two cultures.

Preparing Christmas gifts in our kitchen for distribution to needy families

Another year passed by, but not without much planning and preparation on our family's part. We had to be ready for Christmas, and we began to "get ready" in January. We collected gifts all year, and friends came over from time to time to help us with wrapping. It was not unusual to come to our home on a sweltering day in July and find us wrapping and tagging Christmas packages. Our list had grown to 107 families. We had many needs in order to make Christmas special for the hundreds of people on our list. So many families to provide for, but we trusted completely that God would meet those needs.

2 Corinthians 9:10-13 (NIV) states," Now He who supplies seed to the sower and bread for food will also supply and increase your store of seed and will enlarge the harvest of your righteousness. You will be made rich in every way so that you can be generous on every occasion, and through us your generosity will result in thanksgiving to God. This service that you perform is not only supplying the needs of God's people but is also overflowing in many expressions of thanks to God."

One day, Al and I received an envelope in the mail. It was addressed to us, but both the house number and the street were incorrect. There was no return address. I opened it, and out fell two crisp $100 bills! An unsigned note read, "Use this for your Christmas project for needy families."

Mittens were on sale for ninety-nine cents a pair at a local store, and I bought ninety pair with the money. I also bought blankets and children's pajamas. As

Christmas approached, the school children were busy making special cards for each of the families as well as for the jail inmates. We made each family a special ornament with their initial on it. The senior class at the local high school sold fruit as a fundraiser, and they donated all of the extra fruit to us.

We heard that a fifteen year old girl in one of our families had one wish. That wish was for a pretty dress to wear to church. I went shopping for that special dress, but I wasn't sure of her exact size. I found a very pretty baby blue dress with a delicate white lace collar and lace trim for $17, and I bought it, even though I really didn't have the extra money to spend. When I got home and walked in the door, the phone was ringing. It was my neighbor saying she had the $17 she owed me. I had honestly forgotten that she owed me money. Later, I heard from someone who attended the same church that the girl was wearing the dress in church Christmas morning and that it fit perfectly!

A mentally disabled man on our list had in previous years always given money to someone to buy him a gift so he would have something to unwrap on Christmas morning. The thought of someone having no one to remember him was a painful thought. We knew he wanted a calculator, so we bought him one. One woman wished for some pretty dishes. We heard about that wish, and the Lord knew about it, too. A man received a lovely set of dishes from someone at work and donated them to us, not knowing about the woman and her wish.

As in other years, the Lord continued to show His presence and affirmation in even the smallest ways. We needed fifteen dolls, we had fifteen dolls. We needed three size two sleepers and five size three - that's what we had! One of the items we had was fancy night lights. We made sure each elderly person or shut-in received one. All of the night lights, except for two, were white. Those two were brown. Not that it really made a difference what color each person got, but guess how many elderly men we had on our list that year? How could we ever doubt that we were taking care of exactly the people the Lord intended!

Along my route, I saw two little boys walking down the street. We were in the poorest section of our town. I stopped the car, walked over to them and told them they should not talk to strangers, but to just stand there for a minute. We had put extra gifts in the trunk of the car, and I picked out some toys for them. I handed the toys to them, and they took off running. They ran all the way home, but not without stopping every few steps, turning around and giving us the "gift" of their beautiful, excited smiles. The light that shone in their eyes was a beacon to us on that dark, stormy day!

We finished delivering to everyone on our route and then began knocking on all of the doors in that section of town. We passed out dolls, trucks, puzzles and games, along with candy and fresh fruit to all of the children in those buildings. To sum up our feelings on that day, one little girl said it all. She looked up into her father's eyes and exclaimed, "See, Daddy. I told you we'd have Christmas!"

The following year, once again, our numbers had grown. We were up to 137 families. Thirty-one of them were people who answered an ad I had placed in our local paper for anyone in need of Christmas gifts for their children to call me. There were so many special things about that year. We were able to use two rooms in the local convent in our town to set up a "store" where parents could come and pick out one gift for each of their children. They didn't have to pay for them. One mother came in for a gift for her six year old girl. I was excited as I showed her a beautiful, expensive baby doll. She acknowledged it was indeed beautiful, but she declined it. Instead, she asked if we had a tea set because that's what her daughter had asked for. She chose a plastic tea set over an expensive doll because she wanted to be sure her daughter got what she had asked for!

We had set up thirteen routes and had volunteers help with the deliveries. We distributed all of the gifts by noon on Christmas Eve. Shortly after we returned home, I received a phone call from a man who said he had nothing to give his four sons, ages eight to thirteen , and he heard we might be able to help him. At that point, we were not only out of gifts, we were also out of money. I asked if his boys liked model cars they could put together. He said they did, so I told him to go to a local store and pick out four kits. I also told him I would call the owner to let him know he would be coming. I then called the store and told the owner the man was coming in. I asked how much four model cars would be, and he said $20. Having no idea where or how we would come up with the money, I told him I would be in to pay for them the day after Christmas. As I was hanging up the phone, a man walked up to our door. I noticed a $20 bill in his hand. He handed it to me and said, "The Lord told me you needed this." "For the Father knows the things you have need of before you ask Him." Matthew 6:8 (NKJV)

Time and time again, we had no doubt that the Lord was working right along with us. We were so blessed in so many ways, and our faith really grew during those years. We finally had to turn our project over to the Red Cross because it got larger than we could handle. We continued to have a hand in it though, even after the Red Cross took over. Since that very first year, over forty years ago when we decided to help a less fortunate family, Christmas has never been the same. Providing special gifts for those in need has always been a part of our celebration.

Those years had a profound impact on our children. In fact, it was years later, at our oldest son's wedding reception, when the best man surprised us with his toast. He told about losing everything he owned in a fire. He said he was very depressed and discouraged when our son called him and asked him to go shopping with him. He stated that he had no desire to go, but our son convinced him to join him. He told about how Brian was buying all kinds of things, over $200 worth. He said that made him even more depressed since he wasn't buying anything.

When they got in the car, Brian handed him the bags of everything he bought, saying it was all for him! That was the first we had ever heard that our son had helped his friend who had such a great need. That truly blessed us! Our eyes welled up with tears and our hearts were filled with such joy over our son's generosity.

We know God sees our service to others as worship to Him, and that is why we are here on this earth - to worship Him and bring Him glory by how we live our lives.

## Chapter 6

# Murphy's Law and Embarrassing Moments

Have you ever had a day when chaos seems to ensue?  Have you noticed that when something goes wrong on those days, it isn't just one thing?  Before you know it, everything seems to be going wrong.  Some wisdom from Maxine, the cartoon character, "Sometimes I feel like throwing in the towel, but you know what that means - more laundry."  No matter how bad a day is, even though we may feel like going back to bed and covering our heads, that's not the answer. Instead, we need to look to the Lord for the help we need and to determine what He might be trying to teach us in the midst of the chaos.

One day, the phone rang. At the exact same time, a neighbor was at the door. What happened next? My baby who was sitting in his high chair dumped his whole bowl of cereal on his head and began crying, as the cereal and milk ran down his face. That neighbor happened to be the father of ten children. He went home and must have shared with his wife that I was having a hard day. Later that afternoon, he was back with dinner for us. I was humbled, knowing his wife must have had many days like that, yet she reached out to me.

We had a puppy, and my oldest son was outside playing with him. The dog ran into the road right in front of a car and got run over. My son carried him to the house. He was so upset and said we needed to take him to the vet. I told him that the dog couldn't be helped. He was dead. My son then went out behind the barn and began digging a grave.

All of a sudden, he came running to the house, screaming. I thought it was because he was so upset about the dog. I tried consoling him, telling him we could get another dog. He was hyperventilating and trying to say something. I finally realized he was saying, 'the bees, the bees." He had disturbed a wasps' nest while digging, and he had been stung several times. I proceeded to make a paste with meat tenderizer, and as I was spreading some on his neck, there was a wasp at his hairline, and it stung my finger. Ouch!

Another time, my daughter was playing in an old chicken coop out back. She scratched herself on some chicken wire. I wanted to wash it out but didn't have any hydrogen peroxide, so I went to get some from my neighbor. When I got back in the house, the phone was ringing. It was Al who was working out of state at the time. I set the bottle of hydrogen peroxide on the table. When Al asked how things were, I told him all was well, except that Theresa had scratched herself on chicken wire. At that moment, I heard "glub, glub, glub." Our toddler had climbed up on a chair, somehow got the lid off the bottle and drank the contents. Hydrogen peroxide is not poisonous, so I just had him drink a lot of water, and he was fine.

Our youngest son took music lessons at the School of Music in the nearest city. On the way to his lesson one day, he saw a sign outside a fast-food restaurant, advertising a veal parmesan sandwich for a limited time. He asked if he could have one. I told him he could, and I pulled into the drive-thru lane to order it. The only problem was that I was driving our brand-new large van. I was not used to driving such a large vehicle, and I got too close to the guard rail. I was reluctant to try to get out of the predicament, so we prayed for God's intervention. I trusted that He would get us out.

I asked a man coming out of the restaurant if he would help. He said he would, but he also said he wouldn't be held responsible. My son and I exited the van, and the man got in and proceeded to scrape the whole length of the van on the rail.

On the way home, we stopped at a collision shop. I was thinking it would be no big deal to just swipe a line of paint over the scratch and that the cost would be minimal. The man gave me an estimate of just under $200. I told my son that was the most expensive veal parmesan he'd ever have. God answers prayer, but He doesn't always answer in the way we would like, especially if we get ourselves into messes. That was a good lesson learned for both of us!

Have you ever had an embarrassing moment? I have. We were new in town, and on the first Sunday there, we went to church. On the way out, a lady tapped me on the shoulder, and she quietly stated, "You're losing something!" I looked down, and coming out of the pant leg of my slacks was my pantyhose! I reached down and began pulling on them, and they just kept stretching, getting longer and longer. I captured this in a poem.

# New Woman in Church

New woman in church, just look at her.
She must be something, she's causing quite
a stir.
A tap on her shoulder, a soft voice arose,
"Lady, you're losing your pantyhose."

She reaches down to grab them. They
stretch on and on.
She'd like to crawl into the floor. She'd like
to be gone.
Trying to be perfect, but her imperfection
shows.
Talk about first impressions - oh, well, that's
how it goes!

The next day, I went to the local bank to
open our account, and who was the banker
who greeted me there? Yep - the lady from
church who had tapped me on the shoulder!
Does God have a sense of humor? I really
believe He does!

A couple of years later, I had a new baby
and a toddler, so I was usually quite tired by
the end of the day. I had gone to bed the
night before, leaving a sink full of dirty

dishes. I didn't have a dishwasher at the time.

That morning, my aunt and uncle pulled in the driveway. They lived about a half-hour away, and they often came to our town to shop. It was raining pretty hard. When I saw them in the driveway, I hurriedly scooped up all the dishes and put them in the clothes dryer. I certainly wasn't going to let them see a mess! They came in, and my aunt asked, "Can I use your dryer? My coat is soaking wet." I hate to admit my sin, but I must confess I lied and told her it was broken.

Fast forward a few years. Our two oldest children were in school. When they came home each day, they would come in the back door and drop all of their stuff: book bags, lunch bags, sneakers, coats, on top of the washer and dryer that were right by the door as they came in.

One day soon after they got home, some friends of ours pulled in the driveway. Maybe I'm a slow learner, but I did the first thing that came to my mind. I opened the lid of the washer and shoved everything in it. Our friends came in and said, "We are out shopping for a washer, and we'd like to see what features yours has." I had been caught! I couldn't say it was broken because they didn't want to use it. They just wanted to see it. I had to confess to them that I had shoved all of the kids' things into it when I saw them out the window.

Since this was the second time something like that had happened, I knew it wasn't a coincidence. God was speaking to me, telling me it was okay to be real, I didn't need to be perfect. I never did do that again, but maybe it was because I knew God wouldn't let me get away with it!

# Chapter 7

# Ladies of Grace

A group of ladies, all wearing red hats, were processing through a buffet line of the restaurant where a friend and I were having lunch. Those ladies were laughing and having a grand time. I was recently retired and thought it would be great to be a red hat lady. I knew someone who was, so I called her. I asked her, "What do you do?" Her reply was, "We go out to lunch." "But what do you do?" I asked again. "We go out to lunch and just talk and have a good time," she answered. She told me about a website where I could learn more. I did, and I read their motto. It was "All these years, I've done for you. Now I'm going to do for me."

To me, that was selfish, and I didn't think it would be time well-spent. I was disappointed but knew it wasn't the group for me. (I have since heard of some of the groups giving teas for ladies in nursing homes, and I'm sure some of the groups do other worthwhile things in their communities.).

I often have nights when I can't sleep, and I had just had three of them. I was telling a friend about my insomnia, and she asked what I did when I couldn't sleep. I told her I prayed for everyone on my prayer list. She suggested that the next time I had a sleepless night, maybe I should see if the Lord was trying to speak to me.

That night, I was wide awake, so I said, "Lord, are You wanting to say something to me?" I heard Him say in my spirit, "You want to be a Red Hat lady, don't you?" "Yes, but I can't because it's too selfish," I answered. "Then start your own group," was His response. When I asked what that could be, God said, "The White Hat Society, and have the white stand for My purity." Ooh, I liked that!

The next day, I was having lunch with a friend, and I told her all about my conversation with the Lord and how He had given me the idea for a group. She loved the idea and said to count her in. I asked two more friends to be in the core group, and Ladies of Grace was born. The four of us met throughout that summer and came up with a mission statement, a purpose statement, a key Scripture verse and an agenda for our first year. Our key verse is 2 Corinthians 2:14 (NIV), "But thanks be to God who always leads us in triumphal procession in Christ and through us spreads everywhere the fragrance of the knowledge of Him."

Each month, a volunteer prepares a devotional and presents it at our meeting. We also share how the Lord has been working in our lives since we last met. Any lady whose birthday falls in that month receives a white rose. We do two outreach events each year, and we have an annual retreat, a dinner meeting once a year at a restaurant and a formal tea with musicians once a year. When we have our dinner meetings, someone invariably comes up to us and states that they are familiar with the red hats, but not with the white hats, and they always ask if there is a special significance to them. We are then able to tell them that the white stands for Christ's purity, and we proceed to share a little about our group. We have been meeting for over sixteen years, and God has directed us every step of the way! I believe we are letting His fragrance flow out from us to others.

Ladies of Grace at formal tea at a local mansion

A lady came with her friend to our October meeting the first year. It was our second meeting after the group formed. According to her friend, she suffered from depression. November was her birthday month, so she received a white rose at that meeting, and this really seemed to bless her. The conversation was very heavy that evening with some of the women sharing difficult trials they had faced. I attempted to steer the conversation away from those topics to lighter ones, but to no avail. I didn't want her to get discouraged and not come back. However, on their way home, she told her friend the evening was so inspiring to her because all of the ladies who shared emphasized how God had walked through the trials with them. At that meeting, we had also decided who would get gifts for the different members of a needy family we had sponsored for Christmas. She wanted to get the gift for the baby.

At our December meeting, we wrapped all of the gifts. She was not feeling well so she stayed home that night, but sent a soft, cuddly stuffed dog and another small toy for the baby. That was the end of her involvement with Ladies of Grace.

Two days later, she passed away. Several from our group attended her memorial service and the woman who gave her eulogy said she had recently joined a "faith-sharing group of women" and she was "very excited" about it. She told about her going shopping for a special baby gift. My socks were "blessed off" by her comments because I could see the whole picture. God's hand was in it all, from the previous month being her birthday month and her being blessed by the rose to the heavy conversation that inspired her and her faith to having the special assignment of purchasing a baby gift. That was just the beginning of many special moments through the years with the group.

Another specific example of the Lord's direction is how He tells me which speakers to have at our annual luncheons and retreats. One year, He put Christine Wyrtzen's name on my heart. She is a nationally known speaker, author and recording artist and the founder and head of Daughters of Promise Ministries. I had heard her speak at a large women's conference several years before. I knew the Lord was leading me to contact her. I did. She called me and asked me to tell her more about our group. I told her there would be twelve to fifteen ladies on

Ladies of Grace Retreat

the retreat. I also said I knew she spoke at gatherings of hundreds of women but that the Lord had put her name on my heart. "Well, lately, the Lord has been leading me to speak to small groups of twelve to fifteen ladies," she said. "I'll do it!" She traveled 1800 miles round trip to speak to our little group, and what a blessing she was to each of us

God is so present at our meetings. Just an hour before one of our meetings, the lady who was supposed to do the devotional that night called and said she was unable to attend. The topic for that night was "Adoring God." I had to come up with a devotional right away. God reminded me that ten years previously, someone had done a devotional on adoring God. The devotionals usually aren't printed out, but I had recently gone through our scrapbook, and I had seen that one printed out. I took it out, used it that evening, and all were blessed! God knew I'd need it ten years later, and I was able to put my hands on it right away. It should be no surprise God is concerned about all of the details, especially when we are serving Him.

In celebration of our fifteen years as a group, I planned a reunion that included former members, along with the current ones. I also invited all of our past speakers and anyone associated with our Ladies of Grace group. I had been cleaning out our basement, and in the process, I found some old cassette tapes. One was on the fragrance of Christ by Bonnie Barrows Thomas. Since our core verse speaks of that, I listened to it. It was on our core verse, 2 Corinthians 2:14. It would be perfect for our reunion. I have no recollection where I got the tape, but I felt strongly God was telling me to try to get Bonnie, international speaker and the daughter of Cliff Barrows of the Billy

Graham Association, to come for our reunion.  She came over 3000 miles round trip, and she was definitely who the Lord had picked for our special celebration!

Reunion

We need to listen to God when He speaks to us and directs us because He has everything all planned out.  If it is Him we're hearing, all will work out according to His plan.

# Chapter 8

# My Mom

Since I didn't live with my mom while growing up, I really believe God redeemed those years and gave me some extra special times with her and special memories of her.

My mom, Theresa  was "something else"!  When my friend and I flew to New York City to board the ship we were taking to Europe in 1967, our moms went with us. After everyone boarded the ship, we looked out at all of the people who were on the dock "seeing us off."  Everyone was waving white handkerchiefs or kleenexes.  It was pretty much impossible to identify anyone. However, my friend and I had no problem locating our moms in the crowd. My mom had taken her flowered bathrobe out of her suitcase, and she was waving it high in the breeze. We were so blessed by being able to spot them, and we had a good laugh, as well!

Since I love to take pictures, I often go on what I call "photo shoots." Mom was always so happy to go along with me, and we had great times. It was a grand opportunity to see God's beauty and just enjoying being together.

Mom loved lilacs! Her birthday was in May, and it was always when the lilacs were in bloom in our area. The lilac festival was held during that time every year. She and I would always go to

Mom in her "healthier" days at the lilac park

see them during her birthday week, and afterwards, we stopped for hot fudge sundaes.

As the years went by, it was difficult for her to walk at the festival. We began going to a smaller lilac park a short distance away, still stopping for our hot fudge sundaes afterwards. My mom's health began to deteriorate, and she started using a walker. She no longer was able to manage walking around the smaller park. It was then that I started driving her to a very short road where one whole side of the road was a wall of lush, full lilac bushes. I would park the car, she would get out and walk up along the bushes, enjoying their fragrance and their beauty, then on to our sundaes.

Lilac Row

After two or three years, she was unable to walk at all, so I would put her wheelchair in the back of the car, and off we'd go to that same spot where I would push her up and down the row before going for our sundaes. The last time I was able to get her out at all, I just parked the car near the row of bushes, rolled down her window and picked one lilac for her to smell. I then told her I didn't know what I would do when she was no longer here to go see the lilacs with me. "Oh, honey," she said, " Just put a picture of me on the seat, and go." The year after she passed away, my daughter, granddaughter and I went to see the lilacs on Mom's birthday. And of course, after seeing them, we enjoyed our hot fudge sundaes. Such precious memories!

When she was no longer able to walk, Mom got an electric scooter. She loved to ride it to a little restaurant down the road for coffee. One day, one of the wheels went off the sidewalk, and she got stuck in the mud. She told everyone how two big, burly men came and lifted her out so she could go on her merry way, but when she turned to thank them, they were nowhere in sight. She always said they must have been angels. I believe they were!

Mom seemed to have nine lives. She had many "close calls." On one occasion, she was in Intensive Care, and we were all there at the hospital. She wasn't expected to live. That evening, she called each of us to come close, and she said something sweet and very special to each of us. Our youngest son spent the night in her room with her after the rest of us left. She made it through the night and even showed some improvement.

The next day, our son and his girlfriend told us they were getting married. We knew they were planning to get married, but here was the surprise - they wanted to get married in two weeks! Yikes! My son said he decided while he was sitting next to his grandma in ICU that he wanted her to be at his wedding. Working together, he, his girlfriend, her mother and I pulled it off. They were married thirteen days later in the hospital chapel, and his grandma was able to attend. The reception was held in the conference room of the dementia unit of the nursing home, attached to the hospital! Mom made it out of ICU and made it to the wedding. Six months later, she "danced" with her grandson at the reception following the big ceremony where he and his bride renewed their vows. (He pushed and twirled her wheelchair around with her in it!) She had a wonderful time, and we were all blessed as a result. Then, she was able to be at our oldest son's wedding the following year, and she even lived to see three of her great-grandchildren! God had her days all planned!

In addition to lilacs, Mom loved roses. She always used to say, "Don't get me roses after I die. If you're going to get me some, give them to me while I'm alive so I can enjoy them." On her 70th birthday, we gave her seventy roses, and on her 75th, we presented her with seventy-five roses. She was so blessed by them! However, when she turned 80, we did not continue on with that tradition. She was then living in an assisted living facility, and we felt not only that the fragrance would be overwhelming in that tiny room, but it may have seemed like she was at her own wake!

For her 80th birthday, we rented a limousine, and the whole family joined her as we took her out to dinner. When she was taken back to her room at the end of the evening, one of the men from the facility commented to her, "Wow, a limousine. What will they do for your 90th, send you up in a helicopter?" After that, we always told her that was what we'd do, but she went home to be with Jesus just a few months before her 90th birthday. I also used to say when she turned 100, we'd send her off in a hot air balloon, and she could just keep going up to Heaven!

I am especially thankful that God allowed me to be with her when she took her last breath and went to be with Him! The night she died, I was there spending the night with her. Her breathing became very labored, and she was struggling for air, maybe fighting not to give up. "Mom, if Jesus is calling you, you go," I told her. It was as if she needed permission to let go, because at that point, she breathed one relaxed sigh, and she was gone. She often talked about wanting to live on Easy Street. I wouldn't be surprised if that's her address - Easy Street, Heaven! Mom's favorite hymn was C. Austin Miles "In The Garden." She knew that God walked with her and talked with her and told her she was His own. She knew the sound of His voice to be sweet because she embraced Jesus as her Savior. I know that I will see her again someday.

One day, I was deeply hurt by something someone had done. That night when I went to bed, I looked at my mom's picture on my nightstand. She had passed away almost three years before. As I looked at her picture, I said, "Oh, Mom, how I wish I could talk to you," even though I had already cried out in prayer to the Lord.

I had a difficult time falling asleep. As often happens when I can't sleep, several things kept coming to me that I needed to remember for the next day. I got up and went to the computer desk to get a piece of scrap paper that I kept in a box. I proceeded to write in the dark. I turned on the light when I had to turn the paper over to write more things, and there, on the other side of that paper, was a copy of a poem that my mom had written. It was one that I had made smaller to include in thank you notes I sent out following her death. I had been using scrap paper out of that box right along, and every other piece I had used before had been blank. Her poem :

## My Talk with God

As I walked in my garden, I said a little prayer
I know in my heart He heard me, because I felt His presence there.
I didn't ask for furs or diamonds or worldly things.
I asked for riches of a far more worthy kind.
I asked Him to give you good friends and peace of mind.
We talked about your burden. He said you would not have to carry

such a heavy load alone.
He said to lean on Him every step of the
way.
He will give you strength and courage to
face each new day.
And finally, He told me He would guide you
from above.
And most of all He asked me to assure you
of His love.

How amazing, and what a God-thing that He enabled my mother to minister to me. It felt as if she was talking to God about my pain. And, what was better, it was even in her own handwriting! The next morning, I went through all of the pieces of scrap paper, and there was not another one with that poem or anything at all on it! All of the pieces of paper were blank. Once again, God's timing intersecting with His purposes?

# Chapter 9

# Abba, Our Perfect Father

I was blessed to be able to stay at home with my kids until our daughter went to college. I returned to nursing, but I worked in a mental health facility rather than in a hospital. I spent five years working with troubled kids. God used so many of my experiences growing up to help me in counseling those kids. I met with many kids from broken homes, and I was able to relate to what they were going through.

There was a young boy who was very upset because his father was in jail, and he wasn't going to see him for a long time. He wouldn't make eye contact with me. I was able to share with him that when I was his age, I didn't see my mom for almost a year. He then looked right at me. I don't think he could believe that I really knew what he was feeling. That connection helped me be a support for him in the months that followed.

One little girl that I counseled stands out in my mind. She was angry and sad when she first came in. I asked her if she liked tea parties. She immediately brightened up. I told her we would have a tea party every time she met with me, and we did. Another connection! She was able to open up and share her pain. The tea party was a wonderful tool for me to use to help young girls feel at ease, and several girls really liked to talk over tea. Since this was not a Christian counseling center, I was very limited in being able to share my faith, but I did try to let those little girls know that they were special.

I love to have tea parties, and I have many in my home.  Thank God, there are no restrictions there, and I am able to impress upon everyone who comes to my parties that we are royalty because we are daughters of the King of kings!

In addition to hosting them for friends, I especially love to have tea parties with my granddaughters.  I often have one-on-one parties with them, but a highlight of my year is our annual grandma/granddaughters party when all four of them come to spend the night.  I try to make it extra special for them. I want them to know God's love for them and for them to realize that they are princesses because of who their Abba Daddy is!

Tea With My Granddaughters

When I held my first annual tea party for them, upon seeing the table all decorated with fresh flowers and special china, my oldest granddaughter exclaimed, "Mimi, did you do all this just for us?" My response was yes, indeed, I did, because they are special! My prayer is that all who attend one of my tea parties leaves feeling special and enfolded in the arms of their loving Abba, Father.

Back to those years of counseling young people. Not only was I able to help others through my job, something so profound happened that touched me very deeply. One of my clients, a fourteen-year old girl, was killed in a car accident, along with her eleven-year old sister and a friend. The mom was speeding and went through a stop sign. Such a tragedy!

I went to the calling hours and to the funeral for the girl and her sister. The funeral had already started when a man walked in and stood in back. The girls' father spotted him and motioned for him to come forward. He did, and the father met him in the aisle. They were both sobbing, and they embraced. I didn't know who the man was, but he also went over and embraced the girls' mother, who had been driving the car. He then went up to the altar and began talking. He introduced himself as the dad of the friend who was also killed. He then looked over at the dad and mom of the two girls, told them he loved them and thanked them for all the joy they had brought into his daughter's life. He said she loved to spend time in their home. I was so overcome with emotion to see the display of total forgiveness he had toward the woman who had been irresponsible behind the wheel and responsible for his daughter's death. Never before had I witnessed such evidence of God's incredible grace in action!

When I got home from the funeral, my husband was repairing a lamp for a friend. He was working on it in the middle of the living room floor on the wall-to-wall carpet. When I asked him to please not do it there, he said it wasn't hurting the carpet, but a few minutes later, he called to me and told me I was going to be upset. He had burned about a four inch circle in the carpet, right in the middle of the room. I was very upset, but just for a moment. I remembered those two dads embracing and the total forgiveness I had witnessed just a couple of hours before. I could no longer be upset, and I told my precious husband I forgave him. Ephesians 4:32 (NIV) tells us to "Be kind and compassionate to one another, forgiving each other, just as in Christ God forgave you."

The forgiveness of God when we repent of our sin and of any wrongdoing is a promise He gives us. "If we confess our sins, He is faithful and just to forgive us our sins and to cleanse us from all unrighteousness." 1John 1:9 (NIV). We are called to forgive others as He forgives us. Unforgiveness holds us in bondage, but forgiveness sets us free. It is His grace that enables us to forgive someone else.

Jesus told a parable in the New Testament about the young man who wanted his inheritance from his father, and when he got it, he went out and squandered it. When he finally came to his senses, he went home. His father saw him coming down the road a long way off. The father could have been angry with his son for taking his inheritance and being reckless and foolish with it. He could have been angry with his son for causing him worry and anguish. Instead, he <u>ran</u> down the road to meet him and welcome him home. The father embraced his son, and at that moment, the father forgave him for all he had done. He most likely forgot the anguish he had felt not knowing where his son was or what was happening to him. He was filled with such joy and gratitude that his son had come home, he even threw a party to celebrate.

Our oldest son was in his twenties and still living at home. I walked by his room one day, and it was a mess, so I cleaned it. That evening, while Al and I were out, our son moved out. We realized he must have gotten angry over my "invading his privacy." That was before cell phones, and we didn't know where he had gone.

That was in August, and we didn't hear from him. We prayed. I cried. He did call his dad six weeks later to wish him a happy birthday, but he wouldn't tell him where he was, and then, we didn't hear from him again. As Christmas approached, if anyone had asked me what I wanted for Christmas, I would have told them, "I just want my son to come home."

Our whole family was together at our house on Christmas Eve. I was in the kitchen when I heard one of my sisters say, "Brian is here." There could have been no sweeter words to my ears! I immediately went to the door, getting there just as he was coming in. We embraced, and I cried tears of sheer joy! My son came home! God answered my prayer and made sure I got the only thing I wanted for Christmas.

He has since been a wonderful son through the years, and today, he is a God-loving man with a beautiful family of his own! He really wasn't a prodigal. It's just that out of his being upset over my cleaning his room, he had moved out, began living independently and severed contact with us for those four months. However, I believe God gave me a first hand experience so I would really know, not just imagine, how the father of the prodigal son felt and how

He Himself feels when one of His children comes home!

I know my dad loved me, but his love was conditional. If I behaved, if I did what he expected of me, if I did everything "right" in his eyes, he was happy with me. I always felt like I was climbing up the rungs of a ladder in my relationship with him, and if I made the least little mistake, I would slip down to the bottom and have to start climbing all over again.

How refreshing and freeing when I finally grasped that God, my Heavenly Father, loves me unconditionally! I can't mess up so badly that God, our Father will say, "That's it! I've had it with you. You are a disappointment to Me." He loves me. He loves you - let that sink in! We don't have to do anything or to behave in a certain way to earn His love. In fact, we can't do anything to earn it. It is a free gift, not a reward for something we've done. And He knows us. He knows everything about us. After all, He made us! I have a plaque on the wall that says, "Jesus knows me. This I love." He knows every thought we think.

He knows our motives for everything we do. We aren't perfect, He knows that, but He loves us anyway. In fact, He calls us His Beloved! What an amazing love!

# Chapter 10

# Aging Grace-fully

I am now in the latter years of my life.
Some call these years the twilight years,
others say they are the golden years. My
mom used to say they were the rusty years
since parts of her body were beginning to
ache, and she had difficulty moving around.
However, no matter how old we are, we can
still continue to grow in the Lord and to
fulfill the purpose God has for each of us.
We can be mentors to younger women. In
fact, we all have been called to exactly that
in Scripture. Titus 2:3-5 (NIV) reads,

"Likewise, teach the older women to be
reverent in the way they live, not to be

slanderers or addicted to much wine, but to teach what is good. Then they can train the younger women to love their husbands and children, to be self-controlled and pure, to be busy at home, to be kind, and to be subject to their husbands, so that no one will malign the word of God."

We can share our knowledge of Scripture with newer Christians. We can be encouragers. We can be an example to our grandchildren and pray for them to stay close to the Lord every day. A really good prayer to pray for them is:

"...since the day we heard about you, we have not stopped praying for you and asking God to fill you with the knowledge of His will through all spiritual wisdom and understanding. And we pray this in order that you may live a life worthy of the Lord and may please Him in every way: bearing fruit in every good work, growing in the knowledge of God, being strengthened with all power according to His glorious might so that you may have great endurance and patience and joyfully giving thanks to the Father who has qualified you to share in the inheritance of the saints in the kingdom of light." Colossians 1:9-12 (NIV)

Our grandchildren are being raised to love God. There is no greater joy than that for us as their grandparents. One day, one of our granddaughters, who was four years old at the time, told her mom she wanted to take Jesus out of her heart. When her mom asked her why, she responded, "because I want to hug Him." On another occasion, one of my other granddaughters, five years old at the time, was crying. When her mom asked why she was crying, she said that she had asked Jesus into her heart, but her brother, who is just a year older, told her she did it wrong. Their mom said he needed to work on his evangelism style! When our oldest grandson was three, he had a rash. I told him I had prayed for his rash, and he asked, "Why? Is my rash sick?" That same grandson had buttoned his shirt wrong and I pointed it out to him. His response was "Only God is perfect."

One of our granddaughters, when she was six, was talking to a friend and said, "You should believe in God. Who else could create you?" They get it! Her brother told her she was fired. Her response was," I don't even have a job. You can't fire me." Her brother then said, "I'm firing you as my sister." She shot back with, "You can't because God sent me to you." That same granddaughter was very concerned about someone who was very ill and dying. She asked Al and me to pray for him to come to know Jesus before he died. A friend of mine stopped in while my granddaughter was here one day, and she asked my friend to pray for him, as well. Her precious heart is for the lost!

When our oldest grandson was just seven years old, he composed the following essay. Many live a whole lifetime before coming to the realization that he did at such a young age.

<u>Beginning to End</u>

"Elevator goes up, stuck at the top because doors won't open. (Mother's Womb)
Mechanics help you get out and then you reach the First Floor.

First floor has everything you ever wished for and is beautiful but you are not satisfied. (The World)

Suddenly you see a stairway. It's a long one and you don't know if you can make it. You decide to climb up the stairway. The room it goes up to is dark, filthy, it is just not good. (The Grave)

When suddenly you see another stairway. You decide to climb up then suddenly see a split in the stairs. To the right the stairway continues, except much more beautiful. The steps are furnished and glossed. (Path to Heaven)

To the left is a big red slide. (Path to Hell) You decide to climb up the stairway because you think back to when you were on the First Floor and unsatisfied. "The slide looks fun but probably won't be. I'm going to go up the stairway."

Eventually you get to the top of the stairway where you are finally satisfied by God. It turns out God was who you were missing on the First Floor."

Deuteronomy 5:9b (NIV) says, "...I, the Lord your God, am a jealous God, punishing the children for the sin of the fathers to the third and fourth generation of those who hate me, but showing love to a thousand generations of those who love Me and keep My commandments." How important it is to leave a legacy of faith for our children, grandchildren and all generations to follow. If we live for the Lord, loving Him and keeping His commandments, we can cling to that promise that He will show love to our children and our grandchildren and on and on! What a sweet, precious promise!

Communicating with our grandchildren when they are young often makes us chuckle. One of my granddaughters wanted to play a board game with me. I took one off the shelf and read that it was for ages five and up. She very excitedly said, "Then, we can play it, because I'm five and you're up!" I went to my daughter's house one day, and my grandson, who was ten at the time, was applying deodorant under his arms. I was surprised and questioned my daughter, "He uses deodorant?" He replied, "Don't worry, Mimi. It's presbyterian-free."

Our dentist's wife raised pot-bellied pigs. I was in for a dental appointment, and he told me some baby pigs had just been born and he thought our grandchildren might enjoy seeing them. We took two of our grandsons to see them one day. On the way, I told the boys our dentist's wife's name and explained she raised these pigs. The five-year old asked, "Is there a daddy?" "Oh, yes, he's our dentist," I said. His eyes widened like saucers as he asked incredulously, "A dentist pig?" I could just imagine him visualizing a pig working on someone's teeth!

These should be reminders to us to be sure we are communicating clearly so there is no misunderstanding, especially when we are presenting the gospel to someone or passing on the promises of God!

As we age, it is not unusual to suffer loss. There can be the loss of a spouse or even of a child. There often is the loss of mobility and the loss of independence. But, we should never lose hope if we are walking with the Lord. Someone who recently lost his wife told me, "I didn't just lose someone I loved. I lost someone who loved me." That was such a profound statement and one I hadn't really thought about. What a great comfort to know we can never lose God or His love for us, and we can trust Him to keep His promises. His faithfulness to us is a promise. Isaiah 46:4a(NIV) tells us, "Even to your old age and gray hairs, I am He, I am He who will sustain you." All praise and glory to Him!

# Epilogue

We have just returned from celebrating our 50th anniversary in the Canadian Rockies. What an incredibly spectacular area, showcasing God's amazing creation! As usual, He was at work on so many of the details of our trip. I could write on and on about the breathtaking sights we saw and adventures we had, but I'm only going to highlight a couple of them.

I had made advance reservations at hotels and lodges where we would be staying, and in most of them, I just booked a basic room. When we checked in to one of our lodges, the desk clerk told us we had been upgraded to a deluxe unit, complete with a kitchen and a living room. When we asked how much more that would be, his reply was "nothing". We then asked why we were upgraded, and he said they often will just pick someone who had booked a regular room if there is a deluxe unit available. As if that wasn't enough of a blessing from God, showing us His involvement in our trip, the number of the unit just happened to be the exact number of our street address back home! God went on ahead of us, making all of the arrangements, and we believe it was an anniversary gift from Him.

On one of the days we were there, we were looking for one of the recommended sights. We stopped for directions and found out we were headed the wrong way. We turned onto the next turn off the highway to go back the other way. We then noticed a large sign with a woman's name on it. We decided to continue on that road to see what the attraction was. It ended up being about a ten mile drive up a narrow, winding road, and as we were driving along, going higher and higher, we realized we were driving up a mountain. When we got to the end of the road, we were almost to the top of the mountain. It was absolutely gorgeous up there! Had we not been heading the wrong way and had to turn around, we would never have seen what we saw. Once again, God, our personal travel Agent, was orchestrating a special adventure for us!

One morning, while shopping for souvenirs, I went into one of the shoppes while Al waited outside. He handed me the credit card, and after making a purchase, I put the card in my jacket pocket. I forgot to give it back to him, and he didn't think to ask for it.

We returned to our room, and a little later, we drove back in to town for lunch. It had warmed up considerably, so I didn't take my jacket. He asked for the card when we arrived at the restaurant, and that's when I realized I didn't have it with me. Needless to say, my husband was not real happy with me at that moment!

As we drove back to get the card, a huge grizzly bear crossed the road directly in front of us, and I was able to get some great pictures!  That was such a neat surprise, and we both saw God's hand in the situation.  He turned a negative into a really special memory!

Soon after returning home, we renewed our vows with just our children, their spouses, and our grandchildren present.  I pray we are leaving a legacy of love for them!

Going through life with the Lord, the one who goes before us and walks with us, is such an incredible adventure. We are never alone on this journey and that is reason to praise Him and to place our trust in Him completely.

# Endnotes

Introduction:  God With Us
    1. Dr. Mark Hanby, Amaze Us, O God (New York: Howard Books,
        2013), 9.

Chapter 2: Special Homecomings and Getaways
    1. Linda Anderson, Interludes (Colorado Springs, Colorado; Water-
        brook Press, 2001), 47.

    2. Ibid, 48.

Chapter 3: God in the Big Things
    1. Dr. Mark Hanby, Amaze Us, O God (New York: Howard Books,
        2013), 37.

    2. Ibid, 133.

    3. Lysa Terkeurst, It's Not Supposed to Be This Way (Nashville,
        Tennessee: Nelson Books, 2018), 128.

    4. Ibid, 186.

5. Mindy Starns Clark and Leslie Gould, The Amish Nanny (Eugene,
    Oregon: Harvest House, 2011), 351.

Chapter 4: God in the Small Things
    1. Sarah Young, Jesus Calling (Nashville, Tennessee: Thomas Nelson,
    2004), 243.

Made in the USA
Middletown, DE
02 February 2022

59421041R00102